I0110702

ANGELS

OF

DEATH

EMILY WEBB

Clan Destine
PRESS

TRUE CRIME

This revised edition published by Clan Destine Press in 2019

PO Box 121, Bittern
Victoria 3918 Australia

Copyright © Emily Webb

Originally published by The Five Mile Press in 2015.

All rights reserved. No part of this book may be reproduced or transmitted in any form or by any means, including internet search engines and retailers, electronic or mechanical, photocopying (except under the statuary exceptions provisions of the Australian Copyright Act 1968), recording or by any information storage and retrieval system, without prior permission in writing from the publisher.

National Library of Australia Cataloguing-In-Publication data:

Webb, Emily

ANGELS OF DEATH

ISBN: 978-0-6485567-3-2 (paperback)

978-0-6485567-4-9 (eBook)

Cover Design © Willsin Rowe
Design & Typesetting: Clan Destine Press

www.clandestinepress.net

Angels of Death

Contents

Introduction

This is an updated edition of *Angels of Death*, first published in 2015. Sadly, in the four short years since then, there have been many more cases around the world of healthcare workers killing their patients. Two of those cases – a Canadian nurse who's one of that country's most prolific serial killers, and an Australian nurse who killed two of her patients because they had made complaints about her – are featured in this edition.

It's hard to imagine that anyone in the healthcare industry could have murder on their mind. But even as I was putting the final touches on this new edition, ex-nurse Niels Högel was convicted of 85 murders in Germany. Högel was already in jail for murder, and attempted murder, but his latest trial, which ended in June 2019, was an attempt to find out just how many people he'd murdered and to bring some answers to families of the suspected victims.

Högel stalked the rooms of the hospitals he worked, injecting his patients with drugs meant for heart conditions, just so he could revive them and be a hero. He was known as 'Resuscitation Rambo'.

It's feared that between 2000 and 2005, Högel murdered hundreds of people, aged from 34 to 96. He is now the most prolific serial killer in post-war Germany.

While writing *Angels of Death*, I noticed that the pattern of offending with medical serial killers is often alarmingly uniform. Many of these evil angels worked nightshifts where they were unsupervised, they had personal problems and mental health issues, and there were always red flags that meant they could have been stopped. These flags were typically disciplinary issues that were not shared as they moved from job to job; things like drug addiction, criminal convictions, or clouds over their professional practice.

In many of the cases in this book, the murders could have been prevented had there been more rigorous checks and balances in place at every level, from the hospital right up to state legislation.

Before researching this book, I had not realised just how many healthcare professionals had been found guilty of murder.

Frankly, it is disturbing and only partly because these are only the ones we know about. It could be argued that healthcare serial killing is the easiest type of murder to commit and get away with – for years or, possibly forever.

Serial killer nurses and doctors do not have to go looking for their victims, they literally have wards of captive and trusting victims from which to choose.

Serial murder by healthcare professionals is particularly heinous because, by the very nature of their jobs, they are automatically given an enormous amount of trust. But instead of using their skills and training to save lives and comfort people, they use their positions to violate the vulnerabilities of their victims.

It is an unforgivable betrayal of trust.

Emily Webb
Melbourne, Australia 2019

Elizabeth Wettlaufer

- A Twisted Mind -

Every patient I ever picked had some dementia and that was part of what became my criteria. If they had dementia, they couldn't report or if they reported, they wouldn't have been believed...

– Elizabeth Wettlaufer, Ontario, Canada 2018

These are the words of Canadian registered nurse Elizabeth Wettlaufer who pleaded guilty in 2016 to murdering eight and attempting to murder six more of her patients.

At the time of writing, Wettlaufer is Canada's most prolific serial killer. Her crimes only came to light when she confessed to killing her patients and her extensive interviews with investigators and medical professionals have provided a rare, invaluable opportunity for so much insight into the mind of not only a killer, but a healthcare serial killer.

Wettlaufer's crimes prompted the Canadian Government to establish *The Public Inquiry into the Safety and Security of Residents in the Long-Term Care Homes System* (short-named *The Long-Term Care Homes Public Inquiry*) that started in 2018.

The highly vulnerable women and men she murdered were James Silcox, Maurice Granat, Gladys Millard, Helen Matheson, Mary Zurawinski,

Helen Young, Maureen Pickering and Arpad Horvath. She also attempted to murder several more of her patients.

Wettlaufer's crimes are shocking however the circumstances of how she committed them are all too familiar when compared to other cases of healthcare serial murder. Most of the patients she murdered were at Carresant Care in Woodstock, Ontario. She was eventually fired from the facility because she made too many mistakes with patient care, including administering medication. Wettlaufer was a member of the Ontario Nurses Association which brought a grievance against the dismissal. Carresant Care didn't have the appetite for arbitration so settled with Wettlaufer, resulting in $2000, a reference and a sealed employment file. Wettlaufer was free and able to apply for other jobs with the knowledge that her past would not interfere with her working in another healthcare setting.

Wettlaufer first started injecting patients with unauthorised doses of insulin in 2007 when she was working at Carresant Care. She injected Clotilde Adriano, 87 with additional insulin on a number of occasions in 2007. Mrs Adriano died later in 2008. Her death was not attributed to Wettlaufer but police classified her actions as an aggravated assault against Mrs Adriano.

Wettlaufer told police she'd chosen Mrs Adriano as a victim because she was already an insulin-dependent diabetic so the nurse could get her hands on insulin easily.

That same year Wettlaufer also committed an aggravated assault against Mrs Adriano's sister Albina Demedeiros, who also lived at the Carresant Care home (the sisters were in rooms next to each other). Ms Demedeiros died in 2010 at age 91.

Again, Wettlaufer said she picked Ms Demedeiros because she was already a diabetic and confessed she dosed her with extra insulin several times. Wettlaufer told investigators she essentially "stood back" and didn't help Ms Demedeiros following the injections that caused unstable blood sugar levels.

Maurice Silcox, 84, died on August 12, 2007. Wettlaufer confessed she'd deliberately chosen Mr Silcox, a World War II veteran, because she'd found him difficult. He had Alzheimer's Disease and Wettlaufer told police she felt like it was "his time to go" and she had an "urge to kill him" because of the challenges caring for him and his conduct towards staff.

The document "Statement of Facts on Guilty Plea" from the *The Long-Term Care Homes Public Inquiry* detailed that Wettlaufer admitted she felt a deep sense of guilt after overdosing Mr Silcox because he cried out "I love you" and "I'm sorry" before he died. The shame of her actions compounded when his family praised her for her nursing care of their father and grandfather. She also admitted to police that after killing Mr Silcox it felt like a "pressure lifted from my emotions".

Had Wettlaufer not confessed to killing Mr Silcox no one would have known he was murdered. The cause of his death was originally attributed to complications from hip surgery he'd had the week before.

Wettlaufer murdered Maurice Granat, 84 on 23 December 2007. She told police that Mr Granat had been inappropriate with her and that angered her, coupled with general resentment and pressure over her life and relationship at the time, and she decided to kill him.

Laura Jackson, a close family friend, said that on the night Mr Granat died she'd visited him at the care home and seen the former mechanic "fighting off" Wettlaufer who scurried out of the room when his visitors arrived. Ms Jackson said Wettlaufer stuck in her mind because the nurse was rude and pushy and returned later to inject Mr Granat with "something" (unbeknownst to her, insulin) and he died less that one hour later.

Wayne Hedges, 57, passed away in January 2009 but Wettlaufer admitted overdosing him with insulin a few months before his death, causing a hypoglycaemic event. Mr Hedges was a diabetic who also had schizophrenia and developmental delays and had lived at Carresant Care for almost a decade. Wettlaufer said she made a decision it was Mr Hedge's "time to go" and she claimed he would sometimes mention he wanted to die.

Her next victim was the defenceless Michael Priddle. Wettlaufer attempted to kill him with an overdose of insulin (she couldn't recall to police whether in was 2008 or 2009) and he barely survived the overdose, according to the nurse's statement. Mr Priddle had Huntington's disease, a degenerative, inherited condition. He was unable to speak, had difficulty swallowing and was checked half hourly as he was such a risk for injuries.

Wettlaufer said she got her "surging" feeling the night she tried to kill Mr Priddle, which she took as a sign from God that his life should come to an end.

Gladys Millard was the next unfortunate victim of Wettlaufer. Mrs Millard had Alzheimer's disease and had lived at Carresant Care since 2006. On 13 October 2011 Mrs Millard was on Wettlaufer's patient list during the night shift. Wettlaufer told police Mrs Millard was difficult to care for, including administering medication to the woman. Early the next morning Wettlaufer felt her "red surge" and grabbed insulin from the medications refrigerator and injected Mrs Millard, who was not a diabetic.

Finding a place on the elderly woman's body where she could not push her or fight her, Wettlaufer gave the overdose to Mrs Millard. Covering her tracks, Wettlaufer wrote in her handover notes for the day staff that Mrs Millard had been agitated through the night but was now sleeping and not to be disturbed. When staff did check on her, no one connected that the woman's fast decline – she was sweating, twitchy, pale and her vital signs were low - had anything to do with the "care" she'd received from Wettlaufer. Mrs Millard died in discomfort and stress, her body shutting down for good because Wettlaufer decided to end her life.

The next patient Wettlaufer confessed to murdering was 95-year-old Helen Matheson, a gentle lady who had dementia (but *not* diabetes). Wettlaufer chillingly decided to kill Mrs Matheson after she'd shown an act of kindness to her by bringing the nonagenarian a piece of pie.

The "Agreed Statement of Facts on Guilty Plea" document from the *Long Term Care Enquiry* states '...they discussed Helen Matheson's fondness of blueberry pies and ice cream and how Helen Matheson uses to bake such pies...'

Wettlaufer wrote in her nursing notes: 'she (Helen Matheson) ate 4 bites with ice cream then smiled and said "that's enough dear, but the crust is lovely"...'

Describing her feelings to police about Mrs Matheson, Wettlaufer said she had a rising feeling in her chest before she injected the gentle woman with insulin and then '…after I did it, I got that laughter'.

Mrs Matheson lingered for more than 24 hours and was moved to the palliative care section of Carresant Care, dying with her son at her side. Wettlaufer even looked after her while she was dying, noting 'Helen was flinching and appeared uncomfortable so 10mg (of morphine) was given…' Killed by her nurse, Mrs Matheson wasn't even able to rest in peace, her body exhumed in June 2017 for an autopsy.

Mary Zurawinski had dementia and had only been living at Carresant Care for six months when Wettlaufer injected her with insulin. Telling the widowed mother of four that the needles of insulin were for pain (Mrs Zurawinski was not diabetic) Wettlaufer described again the feeling rising and "laughter" that came after she'd fatally injected the 96-year-old.

Scottish-born Helen Young, 90, had lived at Carresant Care since 2009 and was murdered by Wettlaufer in July 2013. Mrs Young had dementia but not diabetes and Wettlaufer told investigators she was irritated by Mrs Young's constant cry of "help me, nurse".

Wettlaufer decided she'd kill Mrs Young when the woman was asking for help and saying she wanted to die. Like previous victims, Wettlaufer told Mrs Young the multiple injections of insulin were for pain relief. She died the next morning, suffering from the overdose with seizures and discomfort. Later when Mrs Young's upset niece came to pick up her belongings, Wettlaufer comforted the woman.

Wettlaufer knew exactly what she was doing when she gave Maureen Pickering fatal doses of insulin in March 2014, although in her statement to police she claimed she only wanted to place Mrs Pickering in a coma so she'd calm down. Wettlaufer explained she was irritated that she had do give so much attention to Mrs Pickering when she also had to care for many other patients and give them their medications. The 79-year-old Mrs Pickering was in Caressant Care with advanced dementia and needed virtually one-to-one care because she wandered and could also get highly agitated and aggressive. So much so a privately paid care attendant was employed to assist at times to relieve the nursing staff at Carresant. The evening Mrs Pickering was dosed with insulin, Wettlaufer was the charge nurse and busy attending to the whole facility.

Mrs Pickering was transferred to the local hospital after she was found unresponsive and sweating heavily. The hospital determined she'd had a stroke and returned her to the care facility's palliative ward where she died, in much discomfort. The nursing notes described that she responded to touch and voice with moans and eye movements and then deteriorated further over the next few days and passed away.

Wettlaufer had been moved on from Carresant Care when Mrs Pickering died after she'd made an error with administering drugs to a patient. For Carresant Care it was the last straw in a catalogue of concerns held about Wettlaufer. It was revealed later at the public enquiry, sparked by Wettlaufer's crimes that when the Carresant Care administrator was filling out the termination form to submit to the College of Nurses of Ontario, she ran out of room because there had been *so many* incidents of misconduct recorded on Wettlaufer's file.

Wettlaufer found another job at a care home – Meadow Park Nursing Home and in April 2014 she continued her killing spree, fatally injecting Arpad Horvath, 75. Mr Horvath had multiple health issues including dementia and diabetes and according to Wettlaufer's confession, he tried to fight off the nurse as she administered the fatal dose of insulin. Mr Horvath lingered for a week, dying on 31 August 2014.

The killer RN moved on again, this time so she could get clean and sober. Wettlaufer was relying heavily on alcohol and opioids (stolen from her workplaces) to manage the stress she felt about her personal life and work. In fact in her confession she blamed her offending, in part, on stress and the demands of her role as an RN in aged care.

She found work with an agency that provided home-based care and another retirement and aged care home called Telfer Place in Paris, Ontario.

There, in September 2015 she attempted to murder a woman in her

70s called Sandra Towler who was hospitalised after being injected with insulin by Wettlaufer but survived.

The next victim was a woman called Beverly Bertram who was 69 and required care in her home after having surgery on her leg. A diabetic, Ms Bertram needed a nurse to administer intravenous antibiotics via a picc line. Wettlaufer attended to her on August 20 2016 for Saint Elizabeth Health Care.

After visiting Ms Bertram, Wettlaufer turned up unannounced at another patient's home. This person was in the shower while Wettlaufer let herself in, claiming she was looking for an oxygen meter she'd left there on a previous visit. She was actually rifling through the person's medication to steal insulin to use on Ms Bertram. Her motive was calculating; Ms Bertram was a diabetic with her own insulin but Wettlaufer knew that if Ms Bertram died, her medication would be checked. Nothing would seem amiss if her insulin supply was in order and therefore, no one would scrutinise Wettlaufer's actions.

Wettlaufer put insulin through Ms Bertram's picc line and the woman reported later feeling very unwell. In a move that saved her life, Ms Bertram did not give herself her dose of insulin that day and recovered at home. Wettlaufer checked Ms Bertram's medical notes to see that the woman had survived.

Days later she resigned from Saint Elizabeth Health Care. It was a move that displayed some sort of restraint and acknowledgment of the danger she posed to her patients. The agency had told Wettlaufer she'd be assigned to caring for children with diabetes in a school environment. Wettlaufer panicked. She later told police she could not trust herself not to do harm to her young patients.

It was actually a tip-off to police that set them on the path to Wettlaufer. While she was a patient at the Centre for Addiction and Mental Health (CAMH) Wettlaufer had confided information that led staff to report concerns to police about the possible killings of patients in her care. The Centre invited Wettlaufer to talk to a lawyer but when she declined the offer they told her they had to report the information to the police and the College of Nurses of Ontario. This did not halt Wettlaufer's confessions and she continued to disclose information, like a purge, during her stay at CAMH.

A handwritten confession (in addition to the long interview with police in which she confessed all and tried to explain her actions) detailed the patients that died, and didn't die, at her hand.

Wettlaufer matter-of-factly wrote who her victims were, why she targeted them and how she felt at the time of committing the murders. For one of the victims, Helen Matheson, Wettlaufer describes her as "quiet and reserved" and "I'm not sure why I chose her. I was feeling angry an (sic) frustrated about my job..."

There was also additional confession from Wettlaufer to murdering another patient, which would have pushed her victim count up to 15 (nine murders and six attempted murders).

This was publicly revealed by CBC News on 31 January 2019. The national broadcaster found out the information from a partly redacted London (Ontario) Police Report revealing Wettlaufer had confessed to injecting palliative care patient Florence Beedall, 77, with insulin in August 2014 while she worked at Meadow Park care home.

Ms Beedall died an hour after being injected with insulin. Despite police conceding they had grounds to go ahead with a charge of assault with a weapon, the charge didn't proceed. A factor was the concerns of Ms Beedall's family about unwanted publicity.

The confessions saved much time and expense for police and the Crown Prosecutors who would have faced an almost impossible task of proving the murders had Wettlaufer *not* spilled all her secrets in the two-and-a-half hour confession. Most of her victims were cremated but two bodies were exhumed.

That Wettlaufer confessed and has spoken at length to investigators is invaluable to the study of killers, especially those who are in the business of studying the motivations and red flags for healthcare serial killers. Wettlaufer said she confessed to the killings out of fear she would harm children after she was told she would be transferred to work in schools where she'd be helping students, in particular with diabetes (her murder method was death by insulin).

In the small interview room in Woodstock, Ontario, Wettlaufer sits barefoot, in a red top and black trousers calmly confessing to her crimes.

'I did have a sense when my marriage broke up God was going to use me for something…,' Wettlaufer told the detective. (In 1997 she married Daniel Wettlaufer, a truck driver she'd met at church and the pair separated in 2007.)

'After a while…some of the murders…whether it was God or the Devil pulling me…'

Susan Horvath, whose father Arpad Horvath was murdered by Wettlaufer told a media pack after the nurse pleaded guilty that she was traumatised by how her father had died and would never forgive the killer nurse.

'She created all this to get caught…she planned this step by step…she wanted to get caught…' Ms Horvath said.

'I mean if anyone wants to destroy their life, this is how you do it…she just pulled the plug on herself…'

Ms Horvath called on changes to happen to nursing homes – better policy, more due diligence on the hiring of staff and improvements in the administration of aged care.

'I don't want my dad's death and everybody's death to be wasted…we have to make a change.

'I know one thing, my mom is not stepping into a nursing home.'

Wettlaufer received the automatic sentence for first degree murder under Canadian law – 25 years before eligibility to apply for parole.

The ripple effect of Wettlaufer's crimes not only affected family and friends of her victims but also the overall psyche of people (and their loved ones) who would spend the last months or years of their lives in aged care.

At the inquiry Dian Shannon, the then head of Telfer Place, Wettlaufer's last place of employment said; 'Pretty much everyone wants to die before you move into long-term care, given the option'.

'We were trying really hard to create that environment where people felt good about moving into long-term care. She stole that away from everybody, that idea that "this can be OK, I'm not betraying my parents, I'm not betraying my loved one".'

There is a school of thought that Wettlaufer confessed for attention and played on her mental health so she could be sent to a forensic facility rather than prison. Wettlaufer was transferred to Institut Philippe-Pinel de Montreal in Quebec in late 2018.

Canadian-based Podcast *Stat* released an episode on 7 January 2019 of an interview with mental health nurse "Stacey" a former friend of Wettlaufer who provided a perspective behind the headlines about the serial killer.

Stacey told host Karen Wickiam, a retired Emergency RN, that when she found out about her friend's shocking crimes on that news she 'immediately went to the washroom and threw up...'

Stacey lived in the same apartment block in Woodstock and they spent a lot of time together.

'The Beth (Elizabeth) I knew is the one that loved her parents immensely and looked after my dog when I had to travel for work...but this Beth was also a monster and took a lot of lives.'

Stacey described Wettlaufer as outgoing and extremely friendly and the pair would sometimes share dinner and drinks.

'I did see a different side of her and was in total disbelief when I found out what she had done and the crimes she committed...'

She also felt Wettlaufer's transfer to a medium security facility was disrespectful to her victims and their loved ones.

'I just feel like she's getting exactly what she's always wanted, which is the attention she always wanted,' Stacey said.

'Now she's able to do gardening and baking and do all these things that she's always loved to do...

'I don't feel like she's really paid a price for what she's done to these families...It makes me wonder now...whether she is a master manipulator...'

Charles Cullen

- Satan's Son -

Charles Cullen, a nurse in New Jersey USA, had suicidal tendencies from an early age. At just nine years old, Cullen had made his first suicide attempt by drinking a mixture from a home chemistry set. The attempts to end his life would continue for years until he found another way to channel the self-disgust, low self-esteem and depression that had plagued him for most of his life. In fact, Cullen's mental torment and victim mentality belied a rat cunning that saw him prey on some of the most helpless, sick and trusting patients whose families believed they were safe and would be nursed with care and compassion. Little did they know that their loved ones were in grave danger at the hands of Nurse Cullen, who had a compulsion to kill. Cullen was able to hide away by working graveyard shifts in intensive care units. The unsociable hours and inability for patients to communicate with him meant that Cullen could murder easily. There was no one to watch him and there was effortless access to his weapons of choice – prescription drugs.

Cullen is serving multiple life sentences at Trenton State Prison, New Jersey, for the murders and attempted murders of 29 patients – he also pleaded guilty to seven murders and three attempted murders while he was working in Pennsylvania. After he was arrested in 2003, Cullen told investigators that he estimated he had killed between 30 and 40 patients during his 16-year career at 10 healthcare facilities. These are the crimes that he confessed to but investigators believe there were many, many more victims; possibly hundreds.

Cullen tried desperately to hide his dark desires, to an extent, by trying to squeeze himself into a so-called normal life that he had craved since childhood. Divorced with two daughters, Cullen was living with a nurse who was pregnant with his third child at the time of his arrest. This was his attempt to find the love he craved. He told investigators, during a marathon seven-hour interview, that he believed love could halt the sickness in his mind that made him kill.

But Cullen was always a loner and his life was not a success. Neighbours who knew Cullen as a child and young man, described him as socially inept and strange.

Charles Edmund Cullen was born on 22 February 1960 in West Orange, New Jersey, the last of eight children. His family were working class and strong Catholics. Florence Cullen kept the home, as most women did those days, and Edmond Cullen drove buses to pay the bills and feed his brood. Little did the couple know but their little Charlie would grow up to bring shame and shock to the Garden State.

New Jersey (NJ) is famous for musicians Bon Jovi, Frank Sinatra and Bruce Springsteen, among others, but also has a disturbing crime history. Mass murderer John List annihilated his family – mother, wife and three children – in 1971 in their Westfield, NJ home and then disappeared for 18 years. He was arrested in Virginia, in 1989 after a tip to television show *America's Most Wanted* when it revisited the crime and revealed a life-like, age-progressed bust of what List may have looked like.

The state is also home to the first documented lone-gunman killing spree in modern American history. In 1949, Howard Unruh, a 28-year-old war veteran, gunned down random strangers in a street in the town of Camden and killed 13 people, including three children. Unruh died in 2009 at age 88, having spent 60 years in a psychiatric institution.

Tragedy struck the Cullen family when Charles was just seven months old. His father, who was in his late 50s at the time of his youngest son's birth, died and left his wife to struggle alone, raising her children on a pension.

Growing up, little Charles was not popular and was the target of bullies. He was a weedy, pale child and one that teachers and fellow students would have found hard to remember, had it not been for the fact that he grew up to be one of America's most prolific murderers. He was intelligent but odd and this was what attracted the attention of the other children who would target Cullen's weaknesses and inability to connect with his peers and tease him.

Such was his unhappiness with life, Cullen made his first attempt at suicide by drinking a concoction made from a chemistry set. It did not give him the escape he craved so he plunged deeper into a fantasy life and a nihilistic view of the world. He had few friends at Our Lady of Lourdes Grammar School and later, West Orange High School. Further fuelling his dim view of the world was a fascination with the literary works of Fyodor Dostoevsky, the Russian writer famous for *Crime and Punishment* where the lead character, plagued by mental anguish, plots a murder. The protagonist justifies his action by his belief that the murder of a morally bankrupt pawnbroker was for a higher purpose and would make the world a better place. Dostoevsky published his famous book in 1866 after years of prison and exile in Siberia.

Cullen would later try to justify his crimes by telling investigators that he was showing mercy to his victims and ending a 'high pain situation'. The New Jersey newspaper *The Star-Ledger*, exclusively obtained Cullen's 12 December 2003 confession where he portrayed himself as a merciful and compassionate nurse and existed under the illusion that his crimes were a community service. However, Cullen also told police during his confession, as reported by *The Star-Ledger* exactly one year after his arrest, that he wished he had died the first time he attempted suicide as a child.

'You know, maybe if I was nine years old and would have had to die that day, all these lives, including my family, wouldn't be affected in this way,' Cullen told Somerset County Detective Sergeant Timothy Braun.

Another – perhaps the most – significant event of Cullen's young life was the death of his mother when he was 17. Mrs Cullen was killed in a car accident in 1978 and Cullen was said to be devastated. In his senior year of high school, despite his reasonable intelligence, Cullen was not able to complete his schooling and he dropped out and joined the navy at 18 years of age.

Trained as a ballistic missiles technician from 1978 to 1979, Cullen received his first post aboard the nuclear submarine USS *Woodrow Wilson*. According to the Navy Cyberspace website, which provides information on all things to do with the United States Navy, missiles technicians are 'a vital element in the maintenance of strategic deterrence'. So Cullen had an important job to do, one that you could be forgiven for thinking would give the troubled young man a sense of direction and purpose in life.

However, just like in school, Petty Officer Third Class Charles Cullen did not fit in with his navy colleagues who considered the pale, strange teenager a misfit. Cullen was the target of relentless bullying during his time on the nuclear submarine and did not last long on his first assignment. A disturbing incident, which was reported to superiors by Cullen's shipmates, was when the then-20-year-old was discovered in a stolen hospital gown, gloves and mask, sitting at the missiles control panel of the submarine.

In the 2004 *New York Times* article 'Death on the Night Shift', the authors tracked down men who had served with Cullen on the *Wilson* and they reminisced about the very strange behaviour of their now-notorious colleague. Petty Officer First Class Michael L Leinen, who discovered Cullen in the strange outfit, said while he did discipline Cullen, the reasons for his medical garb was never explained, though it seemed to hint at his healthcare aspirations.

A transfer from the *Wilson* saw Cullen on a less stressful assignment on the USS *Canopus*, a supply ship, but this did not help his depression or suicidal tendencies. Cullen made more suicide attempts between 1981 and 1984 and it was this unstable behaviour that led to his discharge from the navy, after serving six years. Interestingly the *Wilson* submarine was decommissioned and struck from the Naval Register on 1 September 1994. By this stage, Cullen, now a nurse, had already killed at least three patients.

Just a few months after his navy discharge, Cullen enrolled at the Mountainside Hospital School of Nursing in Montclair, New Jersey. The nursing school was founded in 1892 and its website shows photos of bright, young, shiny nursing students. Trying to imagine the sickly, slight Cullen as once being a student there is a difficult task. The alumni page reminds graduates to 'save the date' for a Mountainside Hospital Alumni Association luncheon, a gathering the school's most notorious student definitely won't be attending.

Cullen, now 27, completed the three-year course in May 1987 but just a few months before his graduation, his brother James died from a drug overdose. In spite of this traumatic event, that year had more hopeful signs for Cullen than any other time of his life. Not only did he graduate but he also married a computer programmer named Adrienne Taub in July 1987.

Any hope that marriage and the arrival of two daughters would help Cullen out of his depression and maladjustment was short-lived. The marriage was not a success. Cullen had been steadily employed at Saint Barnabas Medical Centre in Livingston, New Jersey, from his graduation until January 1992 when he was fired. Cullen was working in the burns unit of the hospital, where the patients required a very high level of care. It was revealed at his trial that the reasons for his termination were for allegedly tampering with bags of intravenous fluid. The hospital conducted its own internal investigation but police were not contacted at the time.

The couple struggled along until January 1993, when Ms Taub filed for divorce. Cullen admitted to investigators when he was confessing to his crimes that his depression was at its worst that year. Their two daughters were aged four and one.

The year of 1993 was a catalyst year for Cullen. Not only was he served with the divorce papers but his behaviour had become increasingly strange, according to statements his ex-wife made to the judge presiding over the proceedings. The truth was that Ms Taub filed for divorce on the grounds of 'extreme cruelty'.

The exact nature of Cullen's behaviour towards his wife was revealed to the public after the Allentown, NJ newspaper the *Morning Call*, applied for and was granted access to a domestic violence file on him. Many of the incidents were also mentioned in the couple's divorce file, which had already been released to the press. The New Jersey Supreme Court noted in its 2004 decision that 'because Mr Cullen is a serial killer there is a legitimate right of the *Morning Call* and others to have access to the bulk of this file. The reality is there is legitimate public interest…'

Adrienne Taub said in her divorce papers that her husband slept on the living-room couch for three years, was a recluse and never took her out. She also detailed disturbing instances of animal cruelty by Cullen where he would torment the family's Yorkshire terriers to the extent that she and her daughters would be awoken by the pets' terrified yelps. *New York Daily News* reported that a former neighbour said Cullen would often leave his dog tied up outside for hours at a time in extreme weather conditions and that the Society for the Prevention of Cruelty to Animals finally rescued the animal. Cullen was mentioned in the People for the Ethical Treatment of Animals' (PETA) report *Animal Abuse & Human Abuse: Partners in Crime* which details research that acts of cruelty to animals are symptomatic of a deep mental disturbance in people and that those, like Cullen (and many other serial killers), who commit acts of cruelty to animals 'don't stop there'.

Combined with his failed relationship, Cullen was also drinking heavily, as described by his ex-wife in her statements to the court. He also discontinued the medication he was taking for his depression.

The divorce proceedings, his state of mind and his inability to see his children sent Cullen on a rapid descent. Ms Taub filed at least two domestic violence complaints against her estranged husband in 1993 and also a restraining order. The first complaint was in the January when she claimed that her husband's state of mind and access to medications in his role as a nurse could put her and her daughters at risk. After each domestic violence complaint that Ms Taub filed, Cullen attempted suicide.

Just over a month after his first attempt in 1993 to die at his own hand, Cullen took the life of a woman who was initially believed to be his first victim, 90-year-old Lucy Mugavero, at the Warren Hospital in Phillipsburg. Mrs Mugavero was killed with an overdose of the heart drug digoxin, which became Cullen's murder weapon of choice. Digoxin is used to treat the symptoms of congestive heart failure such as shortness of breath and rapid heartbeat. Particular caution is needed when using the drug for elderly patients who often require lower maintenance doses. So for Cullen, the drug provided a quick and easy method of murder in the elderly victims that he killed.

For the Mugavero family, the reason for their loved one's death only became apparent in 2004. The family had never suspected her death was unnatural until the prosecutor's office contacted them for a photograph of Lucy Mugavero to show to Cullen.

'I had closure, but this opens everything back up. It makes it seem as though she died yesterday,' Philip Mugavero, Lucy's grandson told the *New York Times* in 2004.

It turned out that Mrs Mugavero wasn't actually the first person Cullen killed. The first victim he admitted to murdering (and only Cullen knows how many people he killed) was in 1988. In 2004, as he was facing court in New Jersey for murdering 24 of his former patients and attempting to kill five others, Cullen also confessed to the 1988 murder of retired New Jersey municipal judge John Yengo Sr, 72, with a fatal dose of lidocaine, a local anaesthetic. Mr Yengo had been admitted to the burns unit of Saint Barnabas Medical Center for severe sunburn in the days before his death.

Events escalated for Cullen after he killed Lucy Mugavero. A few weeks after he administered a fatal injection to her, Cullen was arrested for stalking Michelle Tomlinson, a nurse he worked with at Warren Hospital – specifically, for breaking into her home while she and her son slept. The harassment began after Cullen took Ms Tomlinson out to dinner. The *New York Daily News* reported that as well as breaking into her home, Cullen proposed to her at work and bombarded her with phone calls. Again, Cullen attempted suicide a few days after his arrest. He pleaded guilty to trespass.

The next years of Cullen's life were marked by more job changes and murders. Everywhere Cullen worked, there was a cloud of suspicion. He left Warren Hospital in December 1993 and it was under suspicion of murder. Cullen had killed 91-year-old Helen Dean, who was recovering from breast cancer surgery, in the September of that year. He administered a lethal dose of digoxin to Mrs Dean as she was about to be discharged from hospital. In fact, Cullen entered her room, asked Mrs Dean's son Larry to leave and then gave her the injection. Cullen was not even assigned to Mrs Dean's room and after he left, Mrs Dean and her son complained to other nurses and doctors about the unexpected medication. The next day Mrs Dean died at home from heart failure.

Larry Dean knew his mother's death was not of natural causes and complained to the county prosecutor's office. An investigation proceeded and a medical examiner and the prosecutor's office corroborated Mr Dean's story about the unprescribed medication and identified Cullen as the offender. This investigation represented the chance to stop Cullen in his murderous tracks, yet the drug digoxin was left off the list of medications that her body was tested for. Cullen and other nurses at the hospital were given lie detector tests. When Cullen was arrested in 2003, Warren Hospital was quick to tell the media and investigators that Cullen had passed the lie detector and that no conclusive evidence had been found to charge him with Mrs Dean's death. Mrs Dean's body was exhumed in 2004 to undergo chemical testing as part of the investigations into Cullen's killings.

Cullen continued to work at the hospital, and the fact that he had been convicted of the harassment of a work colleague and had been suspected of giving a patient unprescribed medication was not even grounds for his dismissal.

Cullen left under his own steam, and in April 1994, started work at Hunterdon Medical Center in New Jersey as an intensive care unit (ICU) nurse. Cullen had again placed himself in an environment where he was caring for the most vulnerable of patients.

His divorce had been finalised the year before and he was able to see his children unsupervised. On the surface, Cullen's life was improving – he had gained a nursing licence to work in the state of Pennsylvania and he had started dating again.

There were more murders in the years between 1993 and 1998 and several incidents where Cullen could have been stopped. In 1997 he was fired from News Jersey's Morristown Memorial Hospital for 'poor performance' and then in 1998 dismissed from Pennsylvania's Liberty Nursing and Rehabilitation Center for 'accidentally' breaking a patient's arm. Cullen, whose mental state was fragile at the best of times, was succumbing to the stressors in his life, which included failed relationships and being forced to declare personal bankruptcy.

At the Liberty Nursing and Rehabilitation Center a nurse took the fall for the death of a patient who, of course, Cullen had murdered, this time with a fatal dose of insulin. Cullen worked at the nursing home for around eight months in 1998. Night-shift nurse Kimberley Pepe was assigned to care for the patient Cullen murdered – an 83-year-old man named Francis Henry. Ms Pepe denied to hospital administrators that she had given Mr Henry any insulin but she pointed the finger of suspicion at Cullen, who had been caring for the other patient in the room. Ms Pepe was fired from her position at the facility and later filed a lawsuit against the nursing home, which was settled out of court.

The *New York Times* reported that the nursing home sacked Cullen following the incident in which a patient's arm was broken, after Cullen had been seen going into the room of the elderly female with syringes in his hand (she was not injected, but her arm was somehow broken).

Time and time again Cullen was able to find work despite his dubious employment record – and always in high dependency wards such as burns or ICU. At the end of 1998 he took on two jobs – one in ICU at Easton Hospital in Pennsylvania and the other as a night-shift nurse in the burns unit of Lehigh Valley Hospital in New Jersey.

Cullen's killing spree continued and it was at Lehigh Valley Hospital, in 1999, that he murdered his second-youngest known victim, 22-year-old Matthew Mattern, with digoxin. Mr Mattern had been severely burned in a car accident. The *Philadelphia Inquirer* reported that when Cullen confessed to this murder in 2004, he said it was to 'end his [Mr Mattern's] suffering'.

Rumours circulated about Cullen and despite being under the radar of the hospital authorities at several of his workplaces, he would often leave before anything could be discovered about his murders.

St Luke's Hospital in Bethlehem, Pennsylvania, reported Cullen to the state's nursing board in September 2002 – he had killed at least five patients there over two years – because they were suspicious that he had mishandled medication. Cullen had left the hospital amid growing suspicions of his conduct and the nursing board embarked on an investigation and shared their findings with police. Nurses who spoke to police shared their grave concerns – which were later proven – that Cullen was the cause of patient deaths while he'd worked at St Luke's and they were upset that the hospital had allowed him to leave and take up employment elsewhere.

The nurses had played detective more convincingly than hospital authorities or the police and had compiled their own notes and theories about Cullen being a killer. Why had he left so abruptly? Why did there seem to be more patient deaths when Cullen was on shift?

Time and time again investigations of Cullen fell short. No links could be established between deaths of patients and the hospitals where he worked. According to the *New York Times* 2004 feature article 'Death on the Night Shift', if Cullen's nursing history had been scrutinised, they would have seen that he had been accused of a patient death at one hospital … implicated in a medical 'mistake' at another. This information should have raised alarm bells and warranted a more thorough look at Cullen. But Cullen had no criminal charges relating to his work or disciplinary actions from state nursing boards so he was able to work unrestricted. New Jersey and Pennsylvania, like many US states, were experiencing nursing shortages in the late 1990s and early 2000s and this made it easier for Cullen to gain employment.

Cullen's last post was his deadliest. He started work at Somerset Medical Center in New Jersey in September 2002. Cullen killed at least 13 patients and attempted to murder two others.

One of the patients murdered by Cullen was the Very Reverend Florian J Gall, 68, who had been admitted to hospital with heart disease and other medical problems. Father Gall had been very ill but the priest was making a good recovery. Doctors prescribed digoxin to calm Father Gall's rapid heartbeat – a normal use of the drug – and a blood test after his last dose of the drug showed normal levels. Father Gall had started to come out of his drug-induced coma. But on 27 June 2003, Cullen took a dosage of digoxin from a medication cart, slipped into Father Gall's room and injected him with the drug.

When new blood tests showed Father Gall's digoxin levels were almost five times the normal and safe level, panic mode set in and the hospital tried an antidote to save Father Gall's life. But it was to no avail. The hospital knew Father Gall's death came from a massive overdose of digoxin but did not mention this to his loved ones, including his sister Lucille Gall, who was also a nurse. Lucille had spent time with her brother at his bedside and was there as staff tried to save him.

Father Gall's family and parishioners were shocked by his death but assumed that ill health and his advancing age were the causes. However, it was Father Gall's death on 28 June 2003 that set Cullen's downfall into motion. Computerised records later showed hospital administrators that Cullen had taken the drug and had also checked the medical records and status of Father Gall.

In his final months at the hospital, co-workers reported seeing Cullen in rooms he was not meant to be in and the hospital's computer systems showed that he was accessing records of patients he was not assigned to, as well as requesting medications for patients that had not been prescribed. The New Jersey Poison Information and Education System was first to alert Somerset Medical Center that a recent pattern of drug overdose deaths at the hospital could be the work of an employee killing patients.

The hospital pondered this information for several months until October 2003, when it contacted authorities with its concerns about Cullen. In that time Cullen had killed five more patients and attempted to kill a sixth.

Cullen was fired from Somerset Medical Center in October 2003. Just two months later, he was arrested on suspicion of murder and the whole, terrifying truth of one of America's worst serial killers started to emerge.

Cullen was at dinner with a female friend when police entered the restaurant on 12 December 2003 to arrest him on the suspicion of murdering 68-year-old Father Florian Gall.

Cullen was also charged with the attempted murder of 40-year-old Jin Kyung Han, whom he had tried to kill a week before Father Gall. Ms Han had cancer and health problems. She survived Cullen's murderous attempt on her life but she later died of cancer.

It was the computerised drug-dispensing machine at Somerset Medical Center that provided rock-solid evidence for prosecutors that Cullen had administered lethal doses of digoxin to patients. The machine recorded the times and days Cullen ordered the drug, as well as the names of the patients who were supposed to receive it.

Somerset County Prosecutor Wayne J Forrest said the data showed that Cullen dispensed digoxin at an 'abnormally high rate' while he was employed at Somerset.

The *Morning Call* newspaper reported on 24 January 2004 that the drug-dispensing machine logs told the Somerset prosecutor's office Cullen ordered digoxin for one patient who was not prescribed the drug, took it and then cancelled the order 'in an attempt to conceal his theft of the drug'.

To dodge the death penalty, Cullen agreed to plead guilty and help authorities in New Jersey and Pennsylvania identify all his victims. Investigators say they will never know how many people Cullen really killed. His memory was sketchy and some hospitals he had worked at had destroyed records that may have revealed more victims. By Cullen's own recollection he killed at least 40 people.

His youngest known victim was murdered at Somerset in May 2003 – 21-year-old Michael Strenko. Michael, a star athlete, had a blood disorder and was in hospital for a spleen transplant. Though it was a serious procedure, Michael was expected to make a full recovery.

A heart-wrenching memorial website made by Michael's parents shows baby pictures and the promising life of the young man who was cruelly killed by Cullen in a place where he should have been safe.

Michael's father, Thomas Strenko, was one of the many loved ones of Cullen's victims who spoke at his sentencing hearing on 2 March 2006.

'For someone to be able to hop from hospital to hospital with these problems for over 15 years defies trust,' Mr Strenko said. 'We are outraged that no one stopped Charles Cullen from murdering my son.'

In a disturbing and deeply distressing scene for the victims' families, Cullen broke his silence of the previous years and started rambling and repeating over and over again, 'Your honour, you need to step down.' He kept chanting the words, despite the judge telling him to stop. Even a white cloth gag with duct tape fixed over it failed to stop Cullen shouting. He kept going for 30 minutes while families were reading out their impact statements.

In another bizarre twist that threatened the justice process, Cullen, who was responsible for taking the lives of so many people, then decided to try to save one.

In August 2006, he donated one of his kidneys to Ernie Peckham, the brother of a former girlfriend. Peckham's mother wrote to the serial killer, begging him to help her son. Cullen had once lived with Peckham's sister Michelle, and he was determined to be a match to donate. Cullen's lawyer, Johnnie Mask, said the kidney donation was a way for his client to 'atone for his sins'.

So determined was Cullen to donate his kidney that he threatened to stop cooperating with the detectives who were investigating his crimes that stretched back to the 1980s. The families of Cullen's victims saw this as blackmail and cowardice on the part of the killer who said he would not appear at his sentencing if he were denied the right to surgery to help Mr Peckham. After a series of meetings, New Jersey Attorney General Peter C Harvey agreed to let Cullen have the surgery but only after he appeared at his sentencing hearing.

'We are victim-focused and have factored in the feelings of the families of the murder victims who are angry and still grieving,' Mr Harvey said. 'They [the families] want the court and Cullen to know how much they hurt.'

At the sentencing hearing, as well as interrupting the judge with his rambling, Cullen would not look at any of the families of his victims, as they tearfully and angrily spoke of their pain at losing their loved ones.

'Charles, why don't you look up at us?' yelled one mother as she clutched a photo of her son in his coffin.

'I want you to die tomorrow so you can meet God tomorrow because you know what? There ain't no doors out of hell, babe,' called the granddaughter of victim Mary Natoli. Deborah Yetter-Medina labelled Cullen 'Satan's Son' for murdering her grandmother, who had dementia and was being treated for anxiety when she was killed.

Cullen was sentenced to 11 life sentences without parole for his 'cowardly crimes'. 'Satan's Son' will live the rest of his lives behind bars.

In 2009, he received his twelfth life sentence for the 1998 murder of retired Pennsylvania steelworker Ottomar Schramm, who Cullen killed with an overdose of digoxin at Easton Hospital.

Charles Cullen's crimes led people to question how he could have worked at so many hospitals. Cullen was never given a bad employment reference, nor was information shared that he was under investigation or fired from different hospitals.

A major flaw in the system of healthcare recruitment was revealed during the investigation. There were not adequate and legal ways for employment checks to be undertaken by healthcare facilities into the people they hired. Nor were there reporting requirements or legal protections for employers who suspected a healthcare worker of negligence, misconduct or worse. If any of the places that employed Cullen had the legal ability to check with his former workplaces then they would have discovered that he had been under investigation or had been fired, which could have stopped his murder spree.

In New Jersey, the Health Care Professional Responsibility and Reporting Enhancement Act (also known as the Nurse Cullen Act) became law in 2005 as a direct response to the serial killings.

The act requires healthcare professionals and bodies to notify the New Jersey Division of Consumer Affairs if they have information about incompetence, impairment or negligence of a healthcare worker. The act also means criminal background checks of healthcare workers seeking licence to work in New Jersey is mandatory.

There has been criticism of this act among healthcare professionals in New Jersey who say it is too extreme and people's careers can be ruined by a legitimate mistake or a simple lack of experience.

In 2013, the American television program *60 Minutes* secured an exclusive interview with Cullen. It was the first time the award-winning news show had *ever* interviewed a serial killer and veteran correspondent Steve Kroft interviewed Cullen, who appeared nervous and pathetic behind a glass barrier.

Recalling the interview for the program's online extra 'Correspondent Candids', Mr Kroft said he wasn't sure Cullen would even answer any of his questions.

Producer Graham Messick said Cullen was the 'ultimate insider threat'.

'It takes a really subversive, devious mind to sort of break all the rules and actually use that to commit the worst crime of all, to kill people,' Mr Messick recalled.

During the interview, Mr Kroft asked Cullen if he got pleasure from killing people.

'No, I thought that people weren't suffering anymore. So, in a sense, I thought I was helping,' Cullen answered.

Mr Kroft said that many of the victims were expected to recover and were not in pain and Cullen replied, 'You know, again, you know, I mean, my goal here isn't to justify … You know what I did there is no justification. I just think that the only thing I can say is that I felt overwhelmed at the time.'

Somerset nurse and Cullen's closest friend at the hospital, Amy Ridgeway was also interviewed for the program and told Mr Kroft that at first she couldn't believe Cullen had done anything.

'He was always early, always on time, crisp. Very serious about getting to work,' Ms Ridgeway recalled.

She said she had considered him a good nurse but when she was confronted by the investigators about the evidence, his real employment history and the damning drug printouts that showed Cullen had been taking deadly drugs from the computerised dispenser, the truth could not be denied.

It was at this point a devastated Ms Ridgeway knew her friend was killing people and she offered to help the police. Ms Ridgeway was crucial in helping police to obtain a confession from Cullen. She recalled that she lied to Cullen and told him that investigators were also looking at her as a suspect in the killings.

'What did you say to get him to confess?' Mr Kroft asked Ms Ridgeway.

'I wasn't very honest with him and there's a part of me, I still feel guilty about that. I was manipulating him a bit. I told him the investigators were also looking at me and how could he think that I wasn't somehow going to be implicated,' she said.

'I remember saying to him, "Who was your first victim?" He started to talk and said it was a long time ago.'

Journalist and author Charles Graeber, who wrote the definitive book on Cullen called *The Good Nurse: A True Story of Medicine, Madness, and Murder*, said, 'We'll never know how many people Charlie Cullen killed.'

'I would be very surprised, as would pretty much everyone I have spoken to with any knowledge of this case if it was not in the hundreds, multiple hundreds,' Mr Graeber said.

Cullen said he was sorry for his crimes during the interview but added chillingly, 'Like I said, I don't know if I would have stopped.'

Megan Haines

- Callous Killer -

Judith "Charli" Darragh says her life fell apart after her mother Marie was murdered by a person who was meant to care for her.

Marie Darragh was 82 and living at St Andrews Aged Care in Ballina, New South Wales. Mrs Darragh had several health issues, however Charli said her mum was cognitively sharp and despite needing assistance with personal care and moving around, was a positive, cheerful woman.

On the night of 9 May 2014, Charli said her mother was in good spirits because her beloved Brisbane Broncos Rugby League team had won.

'Mumma was an avid Broncos supporter, whoever they played I would back the other team and whichever one of us backed the losing team would have to buy the other a $2 scratchie card,' Charli said in an email to the author.

Ringing her mother that night Charli told Marie she loved her "to the moon and back", as she always ended their calls.

That was the last time.

Sometime overnight Marie fell into a coma and was unresponsive when staff found her the next morning.

Another woman, Isabella Spencer, was also found in a coma on the morning of 10 May 2014. Isabella had come to St Andrews after having a stroke that affected her mobility. She'd lived in Melbourne most of her life but was moved to Ballina, which was closer to family, including her brother Don Spencer.

She'd only lived at the facility for three months when she was murdered.

Registered nurse Megan Haines was on the shift from 9 to 10 May 2014 and was the only staff member on at St Andrews. This is not an unusual practice for aged care facilities. As a registered nurse (RN), she was responsible for the oversight and care of the elderly residents.

Haines was born in South Africa in 1967 and moved to Australia in 2000. Haines grew up mixed race amid the political regime of Apartheid. Her mother was white and her father was Indian and she felt her race caused her to be the victim of bullying at school and at home, saying her mother treated her two white siblings better than her.

A registered nurse in her birth country, Haines gained her registration as a nurse in Victoria in 2001 with the then Nurses Board of Victoria. Since 1 July 2010 nurses, as well as other health professionals, must be registered with the Australian Health Practitioner Regulation Agency (AHPRA). AHPRA is also responsible for the handling of complaints made against practitioners and ensures that the health field is regulated across the country. During the early 2000s she worked as a nurse in several facilities around Melbourne's Eastern suburbs, including Caulfield, Box Hill and Ringwood.

Haines had not been working at St Andrews for long, just weeks, when she committed the double murder of Isabella and Marie.

'I use to ring (Marie) every morning and she told me a new nurse had started Nite (sic) shift and she didn't like her one bit,' Charli wrote in an email to the author dated 2 August 2018.

'Mum was a very good judge of character,' Charli said.

'At lunch the next day a few of the residents were talking amongst themselves after lunchtime of how mean this new nurse was, very ruff (sic) handling, pushing and shoving them to and from the toilet to their beds etc. calling them useless etc.'

On the night the women died, Haines, as the sole RN on shift, was the only one with access to the secure rooms where medication, including insulin, were stored. Her personalised swipe card enabled her to enter some of the rooms. The system had been damaged in a lightning strike so the records of who entered weren't recorded. So it couldn't be established immediately whose swipe card had been used but it could only have been a certain group of employees (registered nurses) who could gain entry, including Haines – and she was the only RN on shift that night.

When confronted with these facts, Haines claimed she didn't know the pin code to one of the rooms that held medication and she had to ask some other staff who knew it, therefore trying to cast some doubt on the suspicions about her actions that night.

However it was later discovered in a stocktake that insulin ampoules found in a bin at the facility, which belonged to a male resident of the nursing home (the particular mix of insulin was only used for him), had been taken from the medication room by Haines. She'd slipped them into her pocket to use as her silent murder weapon.

As for motive, the night before the murders, the Director of Care at St Andrews, Wendy Turner spoke to Haines about complaints that had been made against her by three residents. They were serious and Ms Turner outlined the nature of these complaints. Ms Turner revealed the names of two of the women who'd made the complaints to Haines -- Marie Darragh and Marjorie Patterson.

According to court records Turner told Haines the complaints breached the terms of her employment and her professional practice standards. Haines was facing disciplinary action and was invited to a meeting the following week and Ms Turner told Haines she shouldn't approach Marie or Marjorie to discuss the complaints, or enter either of their rooms to give them treatment unless she was accompanied by another staff member.

Marie had complained of an incident where she'd asked Haines for some medicated cream to be applied to her vagina and the nurse told her to cover up as she looked "disgusting".

Another resident, Marjorie Patterson, 88, said that Haines handled her roughly when she was assisting Patterson back to bed after using the bathroom. Marjorie said that Haines's handling of her caused her to injure her ankle, however Wendy Turner couldn't see any signs of injury.

The last complaint was made by Isabella Spencer, (whose name was not revealed to Haines by Ms Turner), who'd asked for assistance to go to the toilet and Haines refused, dismissively telling her to just 'piss in her (continence) pad'.

On the night of the murders Haines, trying not to arouse any suspicions, told a care worker not to bother checking on Isabella Spencer as she was asleep. This was no doubt to ensure that the morning staff would find her victim dead and assume she'd fallen ill overnight.

Most nurses will go through their whole careers and never have a serious complaint made against them. Haines's career in Australia was under a cloud with several complaints in 2005, 2007 and 2008 that now, with hindsight, were ominous. She worked in various hospitals including Box Hill Hospital and Maroondah Hospital, part of Eastern Health in Melbourne. At both these hospitals Haines was the subject of complaints – one for failing to provide care for a patient and another about concerns that she'd threatened to access patient information.

In the case of the 2007 complaint at Box Hill Hospital the nurses' board found she'd engaged in unprofessional conduct. The Maroondah Hospital complaint, also in 2007, about Haines's threat via text messages to delve into patient's records, took until the end of 2011 to come to a conclusion and she was found guilty of professional misconduct.

Further complaints followed that Haines had physically assaulted a patient at a medical facility in Caulfield.

In a precursor to what happened to the women at St Andrews in Ballina, Haines was suspected of intentionally drugging two women, on separate occasions, with insulin. There was also suspicion that Haines did so she could steal jewellery from patients, who would be unlikely to rouse.

Police investigated, even searching Haines's home but did not find any of the jewellery she was alleged to have stolen. They did find some marijuana and Haines was charged with drug possession.

After the conclusion of the Maroondah Hospital investigation Haines was not stopped from nursing but told she would have to provide satisfactory employer reports every three months to the relevant regulatory authority (by this time, AHPRA). Haines had let her registration lapse while the investigation was underway and had to apply again to be allowed to practice as an RN.

With high suspicions about the incident at Ballina, police secured a warrant to monitor Haines's phone calls and text messages for a period of time, starting two days after the two women died.

Between 12 May and 7 July detectives listened to 475 separate phone calls and reviewed 640 text messages.

'Yesterday I went to the library, I went to the doctor; I came home and there's like 10 coppers waiting to search my unit,' Ms Haines told a man on the phone in a conversation that was played in court.

'They didn't find what they came for so they just took random crap,' she continued.

'What's this in association with?,' the man asked.

'Apparently the patients were actually given wrong medication but they are looking for things that are like high schedule, Valium, Diazepam all these things.'

The man replied, 'How were they given wrong medication?'.

'I don't know. If he did tell me the whole story, which I don't think so, I was in shock by then, holding my head. I can't remember,' Haines said.

It was actually her ex-partner who helped detectives build the murder case against Haines.

The couple got together in 2008 and back then Haines had revealed in a conversation with him of her knowledge of how you could commit the "perfect murder".

Richard told her 'There is no such thing as a perfect murder. It's impossible'.

Haines replied: 'Yes there is'.

In an interview with the Channel 7 program *Sunday Night*, the ex-partner revealed: 'She said, "Easy, just inject them with insulin". And I said, "Why? Why insulin" and she said "because when the body dies, it keeps assimilating the insulin and leaves no trace".'

This conversation took place while the couple was watching a popular procedural crime show on television.

In a video police interview of surviving victim Marjorie Patterson, submitted as evidence, a detective asks her: 'what do you remember of that night? What do you recall?'.

Ms Patterson replied: 'I remember…whatever her name is…I can't remember that…whoever she was came in and flashed a torch in me (sic) face and said "I've been told if you can't sleep I have to give you Panadol".'

She continued: 'I said "don't you give me those flat white ones that they use here 'cos I can't swallow them". So she (Haines) flashed her torch into the bowl and said "there you are, they're green and white ones". And they were'.

Ms Patterson told the detective she was asleep 'until she (Haines) flashed the light in my face' when the nurse came into her room and spoke to her about the Panadol.

The detective asked: 'Do you often get woken up to be given Panadol?'.

'Never before,' Ms Patterson replied.

Haines was arrested in the seaside hamlet of Seaspray, Victoria on 7 July 2014 and taken to New South Wales. She'd moved to the small coastal town days after she'd resigned from the Ballina nursing home, amid a cloud of complaints and suspicion.

Representing herself at her first hearing at Sydney's Central Local

Court, Haines applied for bail, saying she needed to be with her two children who 'aren't used to being separated from me'. Bail was denied with the police prosecutor, Vanessa Robichaux, telling the court that there was a high risk that Haines would try to flee back to South Africa with her children and had been trying to get the return of the family's South African passports.

Her children, one in their teens and the other aged under 10 were placed in the care of the state in Victoria after her arrest in Seaspray.

Haines also has an adult daughter, and the younger two children now live with a former partner of Haines and reportedly have no contact with their mother.

As reported by *AAP* (9 July 2014) the Magistrate Les Mabbutt refused bail, stating Haines was an unacceptable risk of failing to turn up at further court dates and that she posed a danger to the community.

Her case was adjourned to Lismore Local Court, in New South Wales, however in October 2016 the trial had to be moved to Sydney. It was found that one of the jury members for the Lismore-based trial had a grandmother living at the St Andrews facility in Ballina. The judge dismissed this jury and then, with the next jury panelled, there was found to be connections with either the victims, their families or with witnesses called for the trial.

There were 15 applications from the jury panel in waiting to be discharged and the judge granted 12 of those for the reasons that they were:

> '...almost entirely associated with members of the jury panel knowing one or other of the witnesses, being a patient or attending the practice of one or other of the general practitioners who are to be called to give evidence, and working for or with a business conducted by the family of one of the deceased...'(R V Haines (No.2) [2016] NSWSC 1825).

The trial began in Sydney on 17 October 2016 and went for two-and-a-half weeks. The jury took four hours to find Haines guilty of two counts of murder. On 15 December Justice Garling sentenced her to 36 years, with a minimum of 27 years. Haines will be first eligible for parole in 2041.

In his sentencing remarks Justice Garling said her crimes were

'...motivated by the offender's selfish desire to avoid the inconvenience and consequences of the investigation into complaints made about her...'.

The Sydney Morning Herald reported that in an affidavit submitted to the court, Haines said inmates at Silverwater Prison, where she was held, taunted her with the name "granny killer" and that she was in fear for her safety.

Victim Isabella Spencer's brother Don told media outside the court after the sentencing: 'I knew I'd lose a sister sooner or later but not under those circumstances'.

Meanwhile Charli Darragh honours her mother Marie's memory by campaigning for better staff to patient ratios in aged care and security measures including CCTV in facilities to try to stop rogue nurses like Megan Haines from harming the vulnerable.

In Australia *The Royal Commission into Aged Care Quality and Safety* started in October 2018, with the final report due in April 2020.

Roger Dean

- Nursing Home Killer -

I'm Roger. I'm one of the nurses and just, there was a fire and I just quickly just did what I can, get everyone out and the smoke is just overwhelming. But, you know, we got a lot of people out, so that's the main thing.

These were the words of registered nurse Roger Dean, 35, to a television reporter soon after a fire ripped through the Quakers Hill Nursing Home in Sydney in the early hours of 18 November 2011.

The images of shocked, elderly residents – their faces smudged with ash – were distressing. The residents lay on ambulance stretchers, scared, wide eyes peering from behind oxygen masks and the layers of blankets that covered their fragile bodies.

Nurse Dean, who had only worked at the nursing home for two months, sat in a wheelchair as paramedics treated him with oxygen. Photos taken by the media throng showed Dean looking blankly at the scene from his wheelchair, his face obscured by an oxygen mask.

Dean had been a registered nurse since 1997 and had a decade of experience working within health facilities managed by New South Wales Health. He was born in Vietnam and came to Australia as a young boy. He started at Quakers Hill Nursing Home in September 2011 and worked two night shifts a week. Dean was on the cusp of completing a law degree that he had been studying via Macquarie University.

Later that day, it would become clear to detectives that Dean was also the person who had deliberately lit several fires at the nursing home which had resulted in the deaths of 11 elderly people.

On 17 November, the day before the horrific event, nursing staff conducted an audit of Schedule 8 drugs (also known as 'drugs of dependence' – prescription medicines that have a recognised therapeutic need but a higher risk of misuse, abuse and dependence) and discovered a large quantity of painkillers was missing. Sometime on his night shift, which started at 10.30pm on 16 November and ended at 7am the next day, Dean had stolen 237 Endone tablets and one Kapanol tablet. Both of these medications contain opiates and are used to relieve severe pain, mimicking the effects of morphine.

When the drugs were discovered missing, the clinical manager of the facility was called in and she did a re-audit, which confirmed the theft. The next step was to phone the police, which the clinical manager did at 10pm.

Dean started his new shift around 30 minutes later and at handover was told about the discovery of the missing drugs. At midnight, two police officers arrived to investigate the drug theft but they were called away to an urgent family violence incident soon after.

The clinical manager, who was still at the nursing home and waiting for the officers to return, had watched the CCTV footage and seen Dean enter the treatment room – where the Schedule 8 drugs were kept – 32 times over the course of his shift the previous evening. Hospital protocol dictates that no one should be alone in that room. However, when it became apparent that the police would not return that night, the manager left. It was 3.43am.

Dean knew he needed to create a diversion that would distract from his crime. If he was found out – and he knew he would be found out – his career as a nurse, and any chance to become a lawyer, would be gone.

Armed with a cigarette lighter, Dean made his way to the A wing of the nursing home. He asked two of the staff members to go on a break to ensure he was alone. Dean knew there was no CCTV in the A2 wing of the hospital. He set fire to an empty bed then calmly walked on to the A1 ward entrance. Here, he set another fire in an unoccupied bed of a room where patients Dorothy Sterling and Dorothy Wu were asleep in their beds. Dean was well aware that both of the women were immobile and would be incapable of escaping the fire without help.

The first fire triggered the fire alarm almost immediately and emergency crews soon arrived at the scene. CCTV footage from that night shows the hectic evacuation. Frail and confused residents – some shuffling along on walkers – were all gathered on the outside lawns, surrounded by ambulances and emergency workers. It was a chaotic scene that looked like something from a movie set.

On his way out, Dean stopped to help a resident Helen Perry leave her room. Despite Mrs Perry's distressed pleas to help save Ms Sterling and Ms Wu from the room where the fire had now taken hold, Dean assured her that help was on its way.

'Don't worry, Helen, just leave them. We've got to get out. People are on their way to get them,' Dean told her.

Mrs Perry later described the evacuation scene to the *Sunday Telegraph*: 'I was in a daze for hours after. It just looked like a war scene. There were people scattered everywhere.'

Dean continued to assist some residents to leave the premises while firefighters were battling to extinguish the first fire he had lit. However, they had no idea that a second fire was burning and that two helpless women were in the room. Ms Sterling and Ms Wu were most likely the first people to die from the fires. By the time the firefighters got to the second blaze, they could hear residents screaming for help and the flames had reached the roof.

Once he had exited the building, Dean hovered outside, helping to usher residents away from the nursing home's main entrance. He had an ulterior motive for staying close though … he tried on three separate occasions to re-enter the nursing home but was stopped each time by firefighters.

On the final attempt, Dean pleaded with the firefighters that he had to retrieve the nursing home's drug books (used to record the Schedule

8 medications), which were in a locked cabinet within the secure treatment room. Dean had access to this cabinet and the locked room and showed one of the officers the keys.

He was given permission to re-enter the building, accompanied by two firefighters but he avoided being in sight of the CCTV cameras. According to R v Dean (2013), 'he gave the keys to one of the officers, explained the location of the cabinet and described the two books. He said, "We need them. We need to get these out".' Unable to open the door to the locked room, the firefighters asked Dean if he could help them, but he refused at first, saying he was an asthmatic and needed Ventolin. Eventually, the door was opened, and Dean removed the drug logs from the cabinet. Dean hastily shoved the books into his satchel and told the officers, 'I need to go home, I need to get Ventolin. I live close by and I really need my Ventolin.'

It was on his way home – with the incriminating drug books in his possession – that Dean gave the chilling 'I'm Roger' soundbite to a reporter who had stopped him.

Dean walked hurriedly to his home, a unit he shared with his ex-boyfriend Dean French, just minutes away from the nursing home, and ripped up the drug books. He disposed of the books in the dumpster at the back of The Cheesecake Shop in Quakers Hill, the business run by Mr French. His actions were witnessed by Mr French, who did not reveal that Dean had destroyed the documents until early 2013. Mr French gave evidence in court on the assurance he would not be prosecuted.

Court documents state that Dean was taken by ambulance to Mt Druitt Hospital at noon on the day of the fires and he 'presented with sooty residue on his face and clothes, pale skin, and generally distressed'.

Meanwhile, firefighters were still at the nursing home. A media pack had gathered and journalists were awaiting updates.

One firefighter gave the media some idea of how bad the fire was, especially for the residents: 'They're confused, some of them are suffering from dementia, they're not sure what's going on. It was a horrific scene. They had to crawl on their hands and knees. The roof was on fire above them. This is a firefighter's worst nightmare.'

By 10pm on the night of the fire, police were confident that they had found the culprit. The focus was on Dean before the fires started when police had attended the nursing home to question staff about the stolen drugs and he had been recorded on CCTV going into the drugs room alone (against protocol) 32 times the night before. CCTV footage showed Dean wandering to and from a number of rooms at the nursing home, which fitted the timeframe of the fires. Two of the nurses on duty that night said Dean had told them to both take their breaks at exactly the same time, which was not standard practice. Dean was arrested and given a police caution at 7.50pm. At 9.50pm he began a recorded interview with detectives. The interview lasted for more than two hours and throughout Dean gave calm and measured responses to the hundreds of questions posed by the detectives.

'I know you won't believe it but it was like Satan was saying to me that it's the right thing to do,' Dean calmly told detectives.

On the cigarette lighter he used to start the horrific fire, he said, 'I took the lighter for the purpose of lighting... I didn't expect to light a bed, I just wanted to light something. I just wanted to set alight to something. It just so happened there was an empty bed and I did it to that...'

When detectives asked him about the second fire Dean said, 'It started just as a small flame and I thought that's OK, like that's containable. I didn't expect it to be so big. It was just something stupid and something that I wish I'd never done.'

'I love the residents very much and I have a really good rapport with them so I feel extremely bad and I just feel evil that I'm just corrupted with evil thoughts that would make me do that,' Dean told the detectives at the end of the police interview.

During a search of Dean's townhouse on 21 November, police found drugs, including some of the stolen Endone and Kapanol tablets, which were kept in containers labelled 'Roger's doctor prescribed medication'. Mr French and Dean had separated because of Dean's abuse of prescription drugs.

While he didn't admit to the theft of the drugs during the police interview, Dean later admitted that he lit the fires as a distraction so that management would not investigate further.

In May 2013, Dean pleaded guilty to 11 counts of murder and

eight counts of recklessly causing grievous bodily harm. Prosecutors had rejected his attempt to plead guilty to the lesser charge of manslaughter.

Psychiatrist Michael Diamond examined Dean's police interview and found that as well as his drug addiction, Dean appeared to have a Mixed Personality Disorder with narcissistic traits. Dr Diamond told the court on the second day of Dean's sentencing hearing that he believed Dean's actions were part of a 'considered plan' that would distract from his theft of the prescription tablets.

Dean certainly sounded like he was a complicated personality. It was mentioned by New South Wales Supreme Court Judge Megan Latham during her sentencing remarks that 'the psychiatrists who saw the offender after his admission to custody also noticed the offender's sense of entitlement, indifference to the needs of others, grandiosity and refusal to take advice and instruction …'

There was devastating testimony from the victims' families, who spoke at the sentencing of their horror, hurt and loss. Some of the families wore pin badges bearing the image of their lost loved ones.

The ABC reported that Dean cried as 'one woman described how she sang lullabies to her mother for days before she died' and 'another man spoke of the terror in his father's eyes before he died'.

Sue Webeck, whose mother Verna died in hospital, said her mother was able to speak to detectives from her bed but died soon after.

'Shortly after that, mum's body shut down and I never heard her voice again,' Ms Webeck said. 'For 11 days and nights I sat with mum watching her body decline. I would sing her the lullabies she would sing to me as a child.'

The daughter of 90-year-old victim Neeltje Valkay spoke to the ABC's *7.30 Report* for an episode that aired on 25 May 2013 – the week that Dean pleaded guilty. Elly Valkay spoke of her mother's last days: 'She knew I was there and she grabbed my hand. She held on very tight. And that was three days and it was horrible. The most terrible time. I still have nightmares.'

Dean was sentenced to life without the possibility of parole. In sentencing Dean, Judge Latham said the number of deaths alone was enough to put his offences in the 'worst-case category'.

'The fact that these murders arise out of the offender's reckless indifference rather than an intention to kill or inflict grievous bodily harm does not detract from these principles,' Judge Latham said.

'The pain and terror experienced by all the victims must have been horrific. For those who were unable to move independently and who faced the prospect of being burned alive, or suffocated by smoke, a worse fate is difficult to imagine.'

While Judge Latham pronounced the sentence on Dean, the courtroom was packed with family, friends and supporters of the victims. They cried and applauded when the life sentence was announced.

Amanda Tucker, the granddaughter of victim Dorothy Sterling, said Dean had ruined her family's happy memories of their gran.

'Our memories aren't of a sweet lady who passed away from natural causes. We had to give DNA to know that was our grandmother. He stole our memories,' Ms Tucker told reporters following the sentencing hearing.

Joining Dean in the NSW prison system's 'never to be released' category is fellow ex-nurse and marine Walter Marsh, who stabbed Michelle Beets to death outside her Sydney home.

Ms Beets, who was also a nurse, was Marsh's manager at Royal North Shore Hospital. Marsh brutally slit Ms Beets' throat and stabbed her because he was angry at her decision not to renew his contract in the emergency ward of the hospital. Marsh's employment status affected his Australian work visa and without a job, he would have to return to the United States and pay child support to his ex-wife.

Almost a year after Dean's sentencing, Anglican minister Geoff Bates, who knew Dean well, gave some insight into the notorious killer's life before his horrible crime.

Mr Bates spoke to the *Sydney Morning Herald* for a first-person piece called 'Night of Infamy' (26 February 2014).

Bates said he had met Roger Dean in 2009 when the church door-knocked in the community and had encountered Dean French. Having shared a conversation with Mr French, the church members left some bible reading materials with him, which he later showed to Roger Dean.

Dean found some connection with the tracts and started to attend church and some fellowship groups.

'He was certainly unusual. He was noisy, and needy. And he was chaotic. I don't think he was understood in his life, and I don't think he understood himself,' Mr Bates said.

'I've seen the footage from the incident and in it he lights a fire the size of a 20-cent piece and moves on. It's not as if he moved in with an AK-47 and shot those people. I would have thought murder was an intention to kill. Even people who light bushfires usually have the intention to harm. This doesn't fit.

'Dean's actions were ordinary and the consequences were extraordinary: extraordinarily horrific. I think Dean got the right sentence. At the same time I don't think he murdered anyone.'

Mr Bates applied his Christian beliefs and knowledge of Dean to try to make sense of the nurse's actions… but how could anyone make sense of the selfishness and desperation that was in Dean's mind that night?

However, Geoff Bates said he believed he had seen evil in Dean's actions.

'I'm convinced I've seen evil. In Western countries we don't talk a lot about evil. It's an old-fashioned notion. But I've seen it in the destruction caused on that day in 2011.'

In 2015 an inquest was held into the fire and the findings were damning of the operators of the nursing home.

It was revealed during the inquiry that Quakers Hill Nursing home did no employment or background checks on Roger Dean before they employed him. Dean had not included his most recent employer on his CV (St John of God Hospital in Sydney) and there was a reason.

The inquest revealed shocking details of Dean's past employment record and past behaviour that infuriated the families and friends of the people he killed.

In another job, Dean had previously stalked a colleague and caused criminal damage to their car by pouring paint over it putting nails in the tyres. He had also turned up visibly drug-affected to a work shift and had to be sent home.

Among NSW deputy coroner Hugh Dillon's findings was a recommendation for Australian Health Practitioner Regulation Agency (AHPRA) to set up a healthcare workers database that would include information about a person's disciplinary history or drug or alcohol abuse that could affect patient and fellow staff safety.

There were many learnings from the inquiry for aged care operators. The Fire and Rescue Service of NSW (FRNSW) issued advice in the wake of its experience at the fire.

Based on the difficulties evacuating the residents from the Quakers Hill Fire, including corridors that were not clear, residents who'd hidden under beds and out of sight making it difficult to locate them and the fact that no call was made to Triple Zero (000) to confirm the fire in the first instance, the FRNSW issued advice to aged care operators after the inquest findings.

These included having a clear emergency plan that considered the 'evacuation of non-ambulant patients, such as those connected to medical equipment' and 'In extreme situations residents may need to be carried or dragged to safety'.

The FRNSW also reinforced the urgency of calling 000 so the right resources could be sent to an incident. In the case of Quakers Hill, firefighters turned up under-resourced because the staff relied on the fire alarm and didn't back it up with 000 to explain the situation further.

It was made devastatingly clear that the Quakers Hill staff were not adequately prepared to do a mass evacuation and the emergency plan did not adequately consider the complex needs of their residents – some were visually impaired, had dementia and limited mobility.

He also recommended better design for aged care facilities including adequate fire exits to accommodate hospital beds and corridors with enough space so rescuers and staff can evacuate people safely. A ramp installed at the Quakers Hill site caused problems for staff and fire fighters while trying to evacuate the residents; it was later discovered there was no permit issued for it to be installed.

In 2018 the families of the people killed by the blaze started by Dean launched a class action lawsuit against Opal Aged Care (formerly Domain Principal Group), the operators of the Quakers Hill Nursing Home.

A similar case to Roger Dean's occurred in the United States where a healthcare worker was accused of starting a fire at an aged care facility. In 1976, a 21-year-old nursing assistant and housekeeper was charged with arson and murder after a fire tore through the Wincrest Nursing Home in Chicago, killing 23 people.

Denise Watson admitted to police that she started the fire when she dropped a match into a pile of clothes in a patient's locker. The smoke from the fire in the room swept through the corridor and into the nursing home chapel a few doors away where 40 residents were celebrating Mass. The frail residents could not evacuate the chapel themselves and staff struggled to get everyone out safely. Most of the fatalities came from shock and smoke inhalation. The nursing home did not have an internal sprinkler system. It was discovered that not long before the blaze, Watson had been told by management that she was being fired from her position.

During the investigation, police discovered Watson had a history of being in close proximity to fires. As one officer put it, Watson had a 'bad history of pyromania'. An arson investigator and fireman recognised her name as they scanned a list of employees of the nursing home. They had met Watson before.

In 1973 there was a fire at the house where she lived and it was declared arson by investigators. In 1974 there were three small fires in Watson's apartment that investigators believed were ignited with nail polish remover. There was another fire in 1975 in the hospital room where Watson was a patient but her roommate told investigators that neither she nor Watson were in the room when the fire started.

The Wincrest Nursing Home fire was – and remains – one of the worst ever in Chicago and the 69 counts of murder that Watson was charged with were, at the time, the most counts of murder ever charged to a single defendant in the state's history. (There were three separate murder counts for each individual death.)

The case looked like a slam-dunk for prosecutors and even Watson's public defender, William Murphy, thought his client would surely be found guilty. However, his client told him that her confession came after hours of interrogation by police. Mr Murphy's strategy was to discredit Watson's confession and say that because she was so mentally fragile and tired she was prepared to confess to anything to get out of the interrogation room. He also had her testify in her own defence, thinking that she would make a favourable impression on the jury.

Watson was acquitted on all counts in November 1977 and a *United Press International* news report described that the young woman 'screamed with joy, then collapsed, crying in her lawyer's arms'. Her lawyer Mr Murphy had told the jury his client was 'a young, nice girl' and innocent of all the charges.

Gwendolyn Graham and Catherine Wood

- The Murder Game -

Female serial killers are not common. The case of Catherine Wood and Gwendolyn Graham is one of the rare instances of female serial killers working in tandem. The US case caused a sensation in the Grand Rapids, Michigan area in 1988 when it was revealed that two female nurse's aides had been arrested for serial murder.

According to a British study of female serial murderers, women who work in partnerships are more likely to target adult strangers and kill them by several methods. However, these partnerships are usually a male-female pairing. The 2009 study by Elizabeth Gurian called *Female Serial Murderers: Directions for Future Research on a Hidden Population*, detailed that lone women serial killers' victims were usually family members and poison was the method of choice.

So Wood and Graham blew the lid off the mould (if a serial killer could ever be described as fitting a mould) of what was understood about female killers.

Catherine Wood and Gwendolyn Graham met in 1986 while working as nurse's aides at Alpine Manor Nursing Home in Walker, a suburb of Grand Rapids. Wood was a supervisor, having worked her way up in the few years of working at the facility. Wood had separated from her husband of eight years, Ken Wood, in 1985 and had no real employment skills, having married at 16 and had a baby soon after. She found a job at Alpine Manor, which required little experience and started to enjoy the freedom of being single again.

Gwen Graham moved to the Grand Rapids area from Texas with her girlfriend. Wood first saw Graham in the lunchroom at the nursing home and the pair became fast friends.

Graham moved in with Wood three weeks after the pair met. At first it was meant to be a housemate arrangement but the women quickly became lovers. After the stifling nature of a marriage she never really wanted to be in, Wood found her relationship with Graham to be liberating. It was not the first time Wood had entered into a same-sex relationship, but this time she was exploring her sexuality without the inhibitions of what her parents or friends would think. Wood was discovering more about herself and a new world of sex and intimacy was revealed.

However, two years later, they would both be facing murder charges, the details coming almost entirely from accounts to authorities by Wood, whose charges were reduced in exchange for her testifying against Graham.

According to Wood, the couple worked together, lived together and partied together. It became a volatile relationship and the women received strange looks from co-workers when they made sick jokes about smothering patients. 'Do them' was the alleged language code the women used between them to plot their next victims. There were even rumours of a 'trophy shelf' at the women's home that had trinkets that Graham had allegedly taken from the victims – jewellery, even false teeth. Wood told authorities that Graham took items from each victim, and one woman, a friend of the pair, later testified that the lovers had shown her items such as an anklet and a balloon that they had stolen from the dead patients. However, none of these trinkets were ever found.

Between January and April 1987, there had been a number of deaths of residents at the home including Marguerite Chambers, 60, who had Alzheimer's disease and had died on 18 January. There was no reason to question the deaths of some of these residents ... until October 1988 when Ken Wood walked into a suburban police station and told police officers about his former wife's disturbing revelations.

By April 1987, the romance between Graham and Wood was over. Graham had begun an affair with another co-worker Heather Baragar. Graham and her new partner moved back to Texas.

Wood had told Ken that she was living in fear of Graham and thought she may be killed herself (though apparently Graham, who was now working at a hospital in Tyler, Texas, and Wood kept in touch on the phone). Wood spilled all to her ex-husband, revealing the murders and how they happened. She contacted her ex-husband in July 1987 soon after she split with Graham and, according to Ken, said, 'You wouldn't believe some of the things we've done.'

The 'things' were the alleged murders of at least five women patients.

Ken, understandably, did not believe his former wife at first. It was 14 months before he went to police with his wife's outrageous and disturbing claims. Ken had promised Wood he would keep her secret. She was, after all, the mother of their daughter. He also said he sensed that Wood held a lot of guilt about the killings and that her psychological welfare was at stake.

'I thought about the families of the victims; so many people were going to get hurt,' Ken Wood explained later. 'But Cathy wasn't getting any better. I sensed a lot of guilt. She couldn't let go of what had happened... I went to police because she needed help.'

On 29 November 1988, the sensational news broke that two former employees of Alpine Manor had been arrested for the murder of at least two people at Alpine Manor – Ms Chambers and a 98-year-old woman. Six other deaths of women at the home between January and April 1987 were also being investigated.

The police department had quietly begun investigating the story that had been brought to their attention by Ken Wood – and the only person who could properly tell them what happened was Catherine Wood.

Walker Police Department Lieutenant Tom Freeman said Ken Wood mentioned one of the patients killed by Graham was a woman called Marguerite who had been suffocated with a washcloth.

'He first came across to me he was trying to get even with his wife but as he continued on with his story there seemed to be some basis for the story,' Lieutenant Freeman said.

Lieutenant Freeman decided to examine medical records at the nursing home before he spoke to Cathy Wood. An extensive investigation was conducted, which involved the exhumation of two bodies, including Marguerite Chambers. The other alleged victims had been cremated. Forensic pathologist Dr Stephen Cohle conducted the autopsies and found no external injuries, though he concluded that the statements given by Wood to the police were believable.

Dr Cohle, who is the Kent County Medical Examiner, has co-written two books on his experiences as a forensic pathologist.

'I basically felt that the statements were valid and that the cause of death in both the women was suffocation and was caused by homicide,' Dr Cohle said when interviewed in 1995 for the television series *The Serial Killers*.

The investigation hinged on Wood. Without her story, there was really nothing else to confirm the shocking story of serial murder at the nursing home.

'Wood was driving the flow of information with "titbits" that led me to believe she may actually be involved in the killings,' Lieutenant Freeman revealed for *The Serial Killers* episode on the lethal lovers.

'I had nothing to go on but Wood's testimony.'

And the 'titbits' Cathy revealed left investigators shocked at the bizarre and callous nature of the crimes.

It was alleged by Wood that Graham had made attempts to murder patients towards the end of 1986 by smothering them with a washcloth, however, Wood claimed that Graham said the victims had been able to put up too much of a fight against her murderous hands. If there were complaints made about these serious incidents, then none were recorded on any files. The reputation of Wood and Graham as respected and much-liked employees was at odds with the strange stories they were telling about having sick fun by killing elderly and defenceless residents.

Wood said that she served as a lookout while Graham murdered the patients by suffocation. According to Wood, the victims, who were all in various stages of ill health and dementia, were targeted by the pair for a very specific reason. The story that Wood told her ex-husband and then investigators is that the women chose the victims based on the initials of their first names so that they would spell M-U-R-D-E-R.

Cathy claimed that Gwen told her she killed to 'relieve tension'. It was described in court – and reported widely by the media – that the killings represented an 'emotional release' for Gwen, who had long been an angry woman who self-harmed through her teens.

When detectives had turned up in Texas to speak to Gwen Graham, she immediately denied any involvement.

'She [Graham] stated it was made up by Cathy, that Cathy Wood was trying to get back at her for moving,' Lieutenant Freeman recalled.

Kent County Assistant Prosecutor Dave Schieber said he did not believe the story when investigating officer Lieutenant Freeman first came to him with Wood's claims.

'It was such an unconventional murder, it was something you'd find in the *National Enquirer*,' Schieber said in an interview for *The Serial Killers*.

'I was very sceptical and frankly, didn't believe it at first.'

Wood even insisted on a polygraph test to prove the murders took place. Lieutenant Freeman said Wood broke down in tears after being told she had passed the polygraph and that he thought it was from relief that she had finally been believed.

On the strength of her former lover's story and the police investigation, Gwen Graham was charged with five counts of first-degree murder and one charge of conspiracy to murder.

Graham's trial started on 13 September 1989. As part of her plea bargain, Wood agreed to become the star witness for the prosecution and testify against Graham, the woman she said she loved more than anyone ever before. In return, two murder counts against her were dropped and she agreed to plead guilty to one count each of second-degree murder and conspiracy to commit second-degree murder.

Wood told the court that Graham had enjoyed killing the patients and seemed to particularly enjoy bathing her first victim in preparation of the dead woman's funeral.

'She was always real happy afterwards and I wanted her to be happy,' Wood said under oath at Graham's trial.

'We were supposed to take turns killing so we could never leave each other,' Wood said.

'They [Graham and Wood] were like parasites and they needed each other,' Lieutenant Freeman said.

Newspapers around the United States ran Associated Press' reports from the trial.

Wood said in court that she acted as a lookout while Graham committed the killings and that victims were also selected (by both women) by pinching their noses to see if they would struggle.

Wood also testified that Graham, who had moved on to a new nurse's aide job in Texas, had expressed via the occasional phone call the ex-lovers still made, a desire to harm the babies in the nursery of the hospital where she worked.

'She told me she liked walking past the nursery and she wanted to take one of the babies and smash it against the window. I had to stop her somehow,' Wood testified without the presence of the jury after Graham's defence attorney objected. No doubt the story of wanting to harm innocent newborns would have been information that could prejudice a jury.

However, a spokeswoman for the hospital in question told the court via telephone that there were no unusual or unexplained deaths during the time Graham was employed and that the accused had no access to the newborn nursery. (Graham had been fired by the hospital when they discovered she was being investigated for the Alpine Manor deaths.)

Graham continued to strenuously deny the charges and her defence team said Wood had made the serial killing story up because she was hurt and angry that Graham had left her and moved on to a new relationship.

Graham's live-in girlfriend Heather Baragar was called as the last witness in the case.

Baragar testified that she and Graham became lovers at the time the murders started in January 1987. Baragar said Graham had joked about the murders saying, 'I killed six people'. She also said that Wood was jealous of Graham's relationship with her and threatened to go to the police if Baragar and Graham moved away together.

Graham was visibly distressed by Baragar's testimony and dabbed her eyes with a tissue throughout.

The prosecutor Dave Schieber said on *The Serial Killers* series that he always believed that Baragar was the crucial witness against Graham, rather than Cathy Wood.

'The live-in girlfriend just laid Gwen Graham out in her testimony,' Schieber said.

'Heather, the girlfriend, recalled the manner of death of one of the victims, Marguerite Chambers, and only Graham and Wood knew the details.'

The jury took five hours to find Gwen Graham guilty and she faced a mandatory sentence of life imprisonment, with no possibility of parole.

Associated Press reports from Wood's sentencing on 11 October 1989 detailed Kent County Circuit Judge Robert Benson's words to her.

'Without you, I'm sure this matter never would have been cleared up,' Judge Benson said. 'I'm convinced that you truly show remorse … I'm also convinced that you are in fact a follower and not a leader.'

Wood was sentenced to 20 to 40 years on each count, but the sentences were to be served concurrently.

Wood's lawyer read out a statement on her behalf after the sentencing: 'Saying "I'm sorry" is not enough. Mere words cannot express the remorse and guilt I'll have to live with for the rest of my life. I was caught up in a mess but do not excuse my action or try to blame anyone for my part of this.'

Gwen Graham and Cathy Wood were both interviewed in 1995 for *The Serial Killers* television series. Graham still proclaimed her innocence.

On Wood she had strong and simple words: 'I hate her, I hate her. She's violated my whole life.

'I'm innocent. I can no more prove I am innocent that they could prove I was guilty. I'm stuck here, I'm stuck because of her word.'

Not everyone was taken with Wood's portrayal of herself as a passive and frightened partner of Graham.

Author Lowell Cauffiel wrote the definitive account of the murders with his bestselling book *Forever and Five Days*. Published in 1992, the book portrays Wood as the mastermind behind the killings. The title comes from a poem written by Wood to Graham that ended with the line, 'You'll be mine forever and five days'. Some speculated that this referred to the number of victims the women killed and also the fact that Wood wanted Graham under her control for good.

'Cathy Wood was diabolical,' Mr Cauffiel said in an interview with Associated Press for the book's release.

'Like the classic psychopath she is able to manipulate people by meeting their needs. The prosecution needed a conviction on Gwen, so she met their needs.'

Mr Cauffiel said the patients killed were all on the night shifts of nurse's aides that Cathy Wood disliked for whatever reason, real or imagined.

'She was having people killed to see how other nurses she hated would react,' Mr Cauffiel said.

Journalist Ken Kolker covered the case when he was a reporter for Grand Rapids Press.

'You look into different cases, you always get a gut feeling,' Mr Kolker said when interviewed for *The Serial Killers*.

'Your gut feeling [here] is, "God, I don't even know if it happened and if it did you wouldn't know who was running the show".'

Even after the trial, prosecutor Dave Schieber had his doubts about the women's story.

'I will never know between the two of them...' Mr Schieber said. 'Gwen Graham was more physical, she was a thug. Cathy was brighter.'

(Dave Schieber died in 2009 of cancer.)

As for the real story of what happened? 'The truth lies somewhere in between,' Lowell Cauffiel said.

In late October 2018 Wood, now 56, was granted parole and set to be released from the Federal Correctional Institution in Tallahassee. She had been eligible for parole since 2005 but had several applications denied.

A last minute stay was issued on 24 October 2018 to keep Wood behind bars until the families and advocates of the victims could make a case before a judge why there should be a new parole for Wood.

The Michigan Attorney General Bill Schuette wrote to the Michigan

Parole Board on 23 October 2018 asking them to rescind the grant of parole to Wood: 'Her monstrous and abominable crimes are unspeakable and far beyond any semblance of civilised behaviour...'

At the time of writing, Wood had volunteered to remain in prison until the appeal over her parole, launched on behalf of some of the families of her victims, was settled.

At a hearing on 18 December 2018, Wood appeared via video link and told Judge J. Joseph Rossi, 'I can just stay right here until the appeal is done'.

Denise Ceccon, granddaughter of victim Belle Burkhard was dubious about Wood's decision to remain in prison during the appeal process.

'She's playing to the judge and that's why she's doing it. She's going to stay there and do whatever he wants for her benefit,' Ms Ceccon said, as reported by the Michigan local television station Wood-TV.

According to the report by journalist Ken Kolker, Wood's daughter was also in court for the hearing but made no comment in court or to the media.

Orville Lynn Majors

- Death Angel of Indiana -

'It's all right, punkin. Everything is going to be all right now.'

These were the words of nurse Orville Lynn Majors to an 80-year-old patient who died moments after he gave her a fatal injection of potassium chloride.

Majors, who is suspected of being one of America's worst 'angel of death' serial killers, was overheard saying these words on 23 April 1994 by Paula Holdaway, the daughter of Dorothea Hixon, who was in the 56-bed Vermillion County Hospital for a routine procedure to remove fluid from her lungs.

According to her sworn statement that was tendered to the court, Ms Holdaway said Majors had kissed her mother on the forehead and moments after his seemingly reassuring words and the injection, her eyes rolled back, and she died.

Ms Holdaway was one of only a few who ever witnessed Majors in the room with a patient as they died. Investigators believe that he could have been responsible for up to 100 deaths during the two years he worked at the hospital's intensive care unit (ICU) in the small town of Clinton, Indiana. The town has a population of just under 5000.

The crimes of Orville Lynn Majors left few in the community unscathed.

Majors, who was known to his friends, family and colleagues as Lynn, was born in 1961, the son of a Kentucky coalminer.

He began his healthcare career as a respiratory therapist (RT) aide at a community hospital in Missouri when he was 19 years old. Over the next few years he continued as an RT aide. However, in 1984, while working at a hospital in Daviess County, Missouri, it was found that Majors did not have the proper professional certification to work in that role. Someone gave a tip-off to the hospital's head of respiratory therapy and she did some checking that revealed there was no record of Majors being certified to work in the role. When confronted, Majors produced a certificate, which the supervisor believed must have been forged, and he was fired.

By 1989, Majors was working as a licenced practical nurse. He was given good reports from his supervisors and was regarded as caring, competent and knowledgeable. However, he did have an unacceptable level of absenteeism from work and had received verbal and written warnings about this matter while he worked at Vermillion County Hospital. Majors had been classified as a nurse 'not for rehire' by hospital administration after he left in 1991 but in 1993, he was rehired.

Majors received favourable evaluations from the hospital after his rehiring, and was deemed to be competent enough to work independently within the ICU, meaning he could be the sole nurse on duty at nights in the ward.

After Majors started working at the hospital the number of patient deaths increased dramatically.

Copies of an anonymous letter, sent to the Indiana Department of Health, were forwarded to local newspapers and tipped off the public that there was a potential serial killer in Indiana.

'Would you want one of your loved ones to be a patient in that hospital with a death angel working?' the Associated Press reported the letter asked.

'We need to stop this nurse and I hope you will help us,' the anonymous letter writer pleaded.

The letter writer also mentioned that a nurse had been suspended and that there were concerns that the hospital was going to cover up the deaths.

The Indiana State Police had already started investigating the worrying rise in deaths after the hospital had come to them with its concerns. Their concerns were *very* real.

An in-house analysis by ICU nursing supervisor Dawn Stirek on the deaths in the department found that an ICU patient died every 23 hours when Majors was working. When he wasn't on shift, a patient died every 552 hours. Stirek discovered from examining staff timecards that from May 1993 to March 1995, Majors was on duty for 130 of 147 deaths in the ICU. In each of the four years prior to 1993, there had been no more than 31 patients who had died.

The hospital suspended Majors in early March 1995, and on 27 April, the Indiana Board of Nursing placed his license on a three-month emergency suspension. (His nursing licence was indefinitely suspended by the board in December 1995.)

There was a lingering question of whether the hospital had done enough to act on the suspicions of Ms Stirek and other nurses about the death rate in the ICU.

The hospital's president John Ling Jr, fell on his sword and resigned on 6 October 1995. Mr Ling later admitted to Indiana State Department of Health surveyors that he was aware of a problem with unnatural and suspicious deaths in November 1994. However, he admitted that he did not take action to prevent further deaths in the ICU until 7 March 1995 when he called the police. Mr Ling failed to notify the department or the hospital's governing body of this action though.

Detective Frank Turchi told the Discovery Channel (for the crime series *Very Bad Men*) that once the letter hit the hands of the media, police were 'bombarded by national news. All the media that you could possibly name were coming in to Clinton, Indiana wanting to talk to me about this investigation and who's killing people and what's going on.'

Betty Blanchard was on a team of medical consultants who were tasked by the state police to look at medical charts.

'I cannot go into this with an open mind. I do not believe that a healthcare provider would wilfully murder patients,' Ms Blanchard recalled she told police.

'Given the evidence I was seeing in these medical records and what was happening to these people clinically, I not only came off of my position but I'd changed it 180 degrees.'

'These people were dying deaths that were not consistent with anything clinically happening with them. They were dying deaths that were unnatural.'

Blanchard told the Discovery Channel that there was something the medical investigation team noticed on the files of the people who died. On its own, it may not have aroused suspicion but there was a peculiarity to a particular note *every single* time it was written: 'Quite [sic] environment provided. Cool cloth to brow.'

This was the consistent notation on all the medical records of the people who had died in suspicious circumstances at the hospital.

'What they were trying to chart was "quiet environment"… but quiet was misspelled.'

This set off alarm bells for Ms Blanchard when she read further on in each of the medical files. The evidence was mounting against one nurse…

While the investigation was underway, Majors moved into a mobile home at the back of his parents' property in Lindon, Indiana. He carried on with life and worked at a pet supplies business. It was reported that Majors was openly bisexual in conservative Indiana. He did several media interviews, including a photo shoot where he was pictured with a woman, named as his girlfriend/live-in lover, and her baby daughter. There were photos of the pair in loving poses in a kitchen, at a local bingo game and of Majors lovingly feeding the baby a bottle.

Majors was arrested on 29 December 1997 at his mobile home. It had taken investigators almost three years to build their case, with police devoting more than 70 000 work-hours to the investigation. A media pack was there to greet Majors as police led him in handcuffs from the court where he was officially charged with the offences. Someone shouted from the crowd, 'Still say you're innocent, Lynn?' to which Majors tilted his head and replied with an awkward smile, 'Yes.' Majors was dressed in a red grandpa top (there was a bullet-proof vest underneath) and baggy sweat pants, and his hair was long, in the mullet-style that was fashionable in the 1990s.

Over the course of the investigation, authorities exhumed 15 bodies of patients who had died at the hospital while Majors was employed. Autopsies revealed that three of the patients' deaths were most likely from injections of potassium chloride.

When police searched an address Majors had lived in previously, they found containers of drugs at his home and in his vehicle. This was a major coup for the prosecution as it directly linked Majors with the 'murder weapon'.

Majors was charged with the murders of seven patients who were aged from their mid-50s to almost 90. Meanwhile, many more families were left with the haunting question of whether their loved ones had been killed by Majors.

The victims' stories were similar – all had entered hospital with ailments serious enough to wind up in ICU, but seemed to be improving and expected to be moved to a general ward. However, within a day of their health improvements, the patients were dead.

Luella Hopkins died on 8 January 1994, aged 89. The retired high school teacher was in hospital for the treatment of pneumonia symptoms. Ms Hopkins' hospital roommate said she saw Majors give the woman an injection but her hospital records did not indicate that injections were part of her treatment.

Cecil Smith, 75, died on 3 April 1994 of heart failure that state investigators believed could have been from an injection of potassium chloride.

Dorothea Hixon, a retired nurse, died on 23 April 1994, aged 80. Her daughter testified that Majors was the only nurse to care for Mrs Hixon in the ICU and that she witnessed him give her an injection when no injection had been authorised for Ms Hixon by doctors.

Mary Ann Alderson, 69, died on 7 November 1994. She was admitted to the hospital with chest pains but was better within days. A nurse recalled seeing Majors at Ms Alderson's bedside, holding a syringe. The woman went into respiratory shock minutes later and died.

Derek Maxwell Sr, 64, came to the hospital with an infected foot, which was being treated successfully, and died on 18 November 1994.

Margaret Hornick was 79 when she died on 23 November 1994. The Italian widow had Alzheimer's disease and was in hospital for surgery on a broken hip. She died less than 10 minutes after surgery. Mrs Hornick's own doctor told investigators that he thought her death was suspicious.

Freddie Dale Wilson was the youngest of the victims Majors was charged with killing. Mr Wilson, 56, died on 16 February 1995. His medical certificate listed pneumonia as the cause of death but an autopsy revealed this was not the case and that an injection of potassium chloride could have killed him.

Majors was charged for the murders of these seven patients, but they are only a small fraction of the total amount of people he was thought to have killed. One man, John Rosza, remains convinced Majors murdered his wife. In September 1994, Ethel Rosza, then 62, was admitted to hospital with nausea. Mrs Rosza seemed to be in better health the morning after her admission but then died suddenly from an apparent heart attack.

'I could not accept the circumstance surrounding her death. There was something wrong there. Something drastically wrong,' Mr Rosza told the Associated Press in a 1995 interview when it became public knowledge that Majors was the prime suspect in the suspicious hospital deaths. Majors was never charged in connection with Mrs Rosza's death but her husband never stopped believing that she was a victim of the killer nurse.

'I told everybody I walked into, everybody I saw, [that] they murdered my wife in the hospital,' Mr Rosza told local television station CBS 10 Terre Haute in a 2009 interview.

Majors' trial started on 7 September 1999 and went for six weeks.

The trial was held in the town of Brazil and headed by Clay County Circuit Judge Ernest Yelton. Jurors from another area within the state had to be chosen because it seemed everyone in the towns surrounding the hospital had formed an opinion on the case. It was simply not possible to hold the trial in Vermillion County because of the closeness of the towns to the crimes – many people had been affected.

It was a major event for the community of Brazil with national media descending on the town. The welfare of the jurors was paramount to Judge Yelton, who, as reported by the *Chicago Tribune*, arranged for local churches and community groups to be paid US$650 per week 'to supply homemade lunches and dinners, overseeing the menu himself'. The enterprising Carbon Baptist Church, seeking to fill its building-fund coffers, made wholesome, homemade food and sold it to hungry reporters and cameramen who were covering the trial.

In her opening statement, co-prosecutor Nina Alexander stated, 'The evidence in this case will reveal a man who took into his hands the kind of power we as a society have decided belongs in the hands of God. This man exercised this power on the sick and the elderly.'

Majors did not testify at the trial. His defence attorney Marshall Pinkus said his client was a scapegoat and that the patients had died of causes related to their illnesses and ailments. The defence never really had any more compelling evidence than Majors' defence that the patients died natural deaths.

There was some disturbing testimony, including some from Majors' former roommate Andy Scott Harris, who said in a conversation the pair once had, Majors had spoken of his disdain for old people. 'They should all be gassed,' Harris testified the defendant had told him. Harris was also a nurse and worked at the hospital for one year from December 1994. Harris also testified that when he was packing to move away, he found a bottle of potassium chloride in the garage of the home he shared with Majors. Harris had testified under immunity from prosecution and had undergone a polygraph test, which showed he was not involved in any of the suspicious deaths at the hospital.

Judge Yelton ruled that the prosecution could not show the jurors the study by nurse Dawn Stirek that linked Majors to most of the suspicious deaths at the hospital. This meant that the state had to rely mostly on its medical experts and the discovery of the potassium chloride containers at places linked to Majors.

Ms Stirek did give testimony, and said potassium chloride was available to Majors. *The Star-Tribune* reported Ms Stirek said that the drug, given without being diluted, could cause death.

'I thought it was bad luck … him being present when the deaths occurred,' Ms Stirek added on 7 September 1999, the day the trial started.

Nurse Judy Wagle testified that victim Mary Ann Alderson was in a good condition before she died. Ms Wagle told the court that she saw Majors go into Ms Alderson's room three times before he pressed the 'code' button to indicate an emergency. *The Times-Tribune* reported Ms Wagle said that on the afternoon Ms Alderson died, she was alert, sitting on the side of the bed and breathing easily.

Another witness, hospital cleaner Rhonda Culpepper, testified that she saw Majors enter Ms Alderson's room with a syringe in his hand.

'He hit the code button about two minutes after he entered her room,' Ms Culpepper told the court.

Tonya Cottrell's father was Freddie Dale Wilson, 56. Ms Cottrell testified that Majors gave her father an injection into his intravenous tubing. Ms Cottrell tearfully told the court that almost immediately, Mr Wilson's eyes rolled back and he died.

Dr Prystowsky, a cardiologist and expert witness for the prosecution, examined the victims' readings on heart-rhythm printouts from monitors and confidently said these showed that the deaths were consistent with potassium chloride poisoning.

The probable cause affidavits submitted to the courts detailed the observations of many of Majors' colleagues about the alleged killer's behaviour. Majors had previously been considered to be an amiable, caring nurse, but his colleagues said that in July 1994, which marked the start of the 'epidemic' of killings, Majors 'underwent a personality change'. Two nurses told investigators that Majors began to be much more irritable, 'wild-eyed and almost uncontrollably irate … this was especially true when he felt that things did not go his way or someone criticised him …'

There was a frustrating (and chilling) absence of motive for the killings. In all the court documents and trial testimony, it was still not clear who Orville Lynn Majors *really* was and why he was motivated to kill. There was some speculation that Majors may have been taking drugs, which would account for his change in temperament and lack of patience, but this was never definitively proven.

The discovery of potassium chloride packaging at Major's residence was the most damning evidence for the jury to consider.

A hospital pharmacy technician Debra Feller was another witness for the prosecution and *The Times-Tribune* reported that she identified the drug packages found at his former property as ones that she personally made up for the ICU. As reported by the newspaper, Ms Feller told the court she had noticed drug stocks missing from the ICU and in 1994, when she began ordering more potassium chloride than ever before, she had reported it to her manager.

When the prosecution rested its case, defence attorney Mr Pinkus remarked, 'My gut feeling, as I stand here today, is that this is one of the weakest allegations of murder I have ever seen.'

Majors was found guilty of the murders of six patients. The jury was unable to reach a unanimous verdict in the death of Cyril Smith.

On 15 November 1999, Majors was sentenced to 360 years in prison – 60 years for each of the people he murdered. The *Chicago Tribune* reported that just prior to handing down the sentence, Judge Yelton said, 'Mr Majors' character is indeed an enigma. Certain testimony during the trial painted him with a caring and compassionate brush. But then the canvas turns as black as a moonless night as he killed one human being after another. It is a facet of his character that defies mortal comprehension.'

Yelton continued. 'When a nurse does wrong, he is the worst of criminals. He was entrusted with these people's care. In response, he committed diabolical acts that extinguished the frail lives of six people.'

In the United States, jury members are permitted to speak to the media, and due to the high profile of the Majors case, people were very interested in the thoughts of the 12 men and women who held the serial killer's future in their hands.

In an interview with *Tribune-Star* reporter Mike Ricketts, jurors said it was the state's expert medical witnesses Eric Prystowsky and Bruce Waller who convinced them of Majors' guilt.

Juror Richard Brown said the defence 'never put an expert on the stand that was qualified to challenge' the prosecution's medical experts.

Majors maintained his innocence and his defence team said it would appeal the sentence.

'I absolutely don't believe he killed anyone,' said Majors' attorney. 'These were all very, very sick people.'

Prosecutor Greg Carter said while the guilty verdict was a relief, it was cold comfort to families.

'Justice can never completely be done in this case because these people are dead, and they can never be with their families again,' Mr Carter said.

Nurse Dawn Stirek, whose suspicions kicked off the investigation and eventual trial and punishment of Majors, recalled her shock at what had happened in a television interview several years later.

'Lynn was a good nurse. People liked him. I liked him. I still do.'

The Majors case sparked several important changes within Indiana hospitals to increase patient safety and security. Undiluted potassium chloride is no longer freely available to ward staff and the drug is now pre-mixed in hospital pharmacies.

Co-prosecutors Alexander and Carter believed the Majors case was an eye-opener for hospital administrators throughout the United States.

Veteran *Tribune-Star* journalist Patricia L Pastore, who covered the case from the start, wrote that the discovery of the potassium chloride containers was 'the smoking gun' in the case. In her dissection of the court case, post-sentence, Pastore said that this evidence had been integral to the prosecution, who had played a careful strategy in bringing Majors to trial.

'…The trial became, in many ways, a "battle of the experts" wherein Doctors A, B, C and D for the state said the deaths were foul play, while Doctors W, X, Y and Z for the defence testified with the same vigour and determination that they were the result of natural causes …', the venerable Pastore wrote in her opinion editorial 'Defense chooses to ignore the "smoking gun"', published on 18 December 1999.

In 2002, Majors' legal team launched an appeal that alleged that some jury members had acted inappropriately during the 1999 trial. The appeal *Majors v State of Indiana* mentioned that one juror was seen to make 'inappropriate facial expressions' at a defence attorney.

In August 2002, the Indiana Supreme Court upheld Majors' convictions.

Majors also wanted a new trial because he said jurors had drunk beer during lunch breaks at the trial and drank during deliberations (which went for three days). He also claimed jurors socialised with members of state police at a picnic organised by the Clay County Sheriff. Majors' defence team was pushing for a new trial. However, the appeal court dismissed the claims. In the case of the social gatherings, the appeal judges stated that 'none of the officers at the cookout were involved with the investigation of Majors in any capacity' and the 'Clay County's sheriff ... was a veteran officer who was well versed on appropriate juror exposure and had no involvement in the Majors investigation or prosecution'.

The hospital rebranded in 1996, prior to Majors' trial, as West Central Community Hospital and is now called Union Hospital Clinton.

Majors died aged 56 in the Indiana State Prison on 24 September 2017. *The Tribune Star*, an Indiana regional newspaper reported that Majors died of cardiac issues with death due to natural causes.

Majors never admitted guilt and took the reasons for committing the murders, thought to be of up to 130 people, to the grave – an unsatisfying outcome to many of his victims' families and friends.

The lead investigator on the case, Frank Turchi, reflected on the news of Majors' death for a report on WTWO, an NBC-affiliated television station based in Terra Haute, Indiana.

'We concluded a lot of it was that he considered himself making the decision on their quality of life,' Mr Turchi said.

Genene Jones

- Death in Texas -

Genene Jones could be one of the most prolific child killers in United States' history.

Jones, currently serving a life term in a Texas prison for the murder of a 15-month-old girl, is suspected to have been responsible for the deaths of almost 50 children while she was working as a nurse in several healthcare settings. However, hospital mismanagement and failure to properly investigate serious suspicions about Jones means that she has not been held to account.

Genene Jones was born on 13 July 1950, and adopted. Her adoptive parents also adopted three other children, one older and two younger. As a child, Jones apparently feigned illnesses to get attention.

After graduating from school, Jones became a beautician. She also married – she and her husband were together for four years and had two children, before divorcing. Jones ended up leaving her two children in the care of her adoptive mother.

Jones became a licensed vocational nurse (LVN) in 1977 and started work at the Bexar (pronounced 'bear') County Medical Center Hospital in San Antonio as an LVN in 1978. In Texas, an LVN does one year of study as opposed to a registered nurse, where the qualification is at least two years. Jones thrived on the environment of the paediatric intensive care unit (ICU).

According to people who worked with Jones, she was intelligent, but also straight-talking, bossy and quite coarse, and would always project an attitude of being higher than her station. In fact, Jones acted like she was in charge of the ICU. She was a person who polarised her co-workers. Some doctors and nurses respected her confidence, work ethic and dedication to the patients. However, many, including weary doctors who would be besieged by Jones's 'concerns' about her tiny patients, disliked Jones and saw her as a disruptive influence in the ICU. She became known as an attention seeker and always sought out the sickest babies to care for.

'She pretty much made her own assignment,' nurse Cherlyn Pendergraft told writer Peter Elkind for his 1983 *Texas Monthly* feature article on Jones titled The Death Shift. 'She was so strong she ran like a charge nurse. She was just an LVN. She had no authority or power to do it, but she did it anyway.'

There was always a drama when Genene was around. In fact, the shift she worked – 3pm to 11pm – became known as 'the death shift' among the hospital staff. There had been a noticeable increase in the number of medical emergencies in the ICU during that shift – babies went into cardiac arrest, respiratory distress, had seizures and came close to death. Many did die. The common denominator was that Genene Jones was on duty and she was the one who was caring for these children at the time of their medical emergencies.

Jones seemed to thrive on drama and the tragedy of the babies' deaths, often insisting she take them to the morgue where she would say her goodbyes and cuddle them.

There were some who strongly suspected Jones was harming the babies and creating the medical emergencies so that she could play the hero. Registered nurse Suzanna Maldonado began making a list of all the babies who died during 'the death shift' between 1981 and 1982. She was a relatively newly qualified registered nurse and had worked the shift immediately after Jones's, 11pm to 7am, and wondered why the babies on Jones's shift would be getting even sicker, or even dying. Ms Maldonado took her concerns to her nursing supervisor Pat Belko.

However, the young nurse was advised to stop playing amateur sleuth and leave the matter alone.

Unable to ignore the baby deaths and medical emergencies in the ICU, the hospital conducted its own investigation. The hospital's malpractice attorney had advised a group of senior doctors and board members that to fire the nurse now believed by several to be at the centre of the deaths would create problems. Jones could sue them, which could prove costly and place too much attention on the hospital. Some doctors believed that the problem stemmed from poor leadership from within the ICU.

It was decided that the administrators should press on with the internal investigation but keep the matter under wraps. A report concluded that between May and November 1981, 10 children died from complications that were unexpected and unexplained. In all the cases Genene Jones was at the children's bedsides when they died. In his article, Peter Elkind noted that the report concluded: 'This association of Nurse Jones with the deaths of the ten children could be coincidental. However, negligence or wrongdoing cannot be excluded…'

Soon after, Jones was released from the ICU by the Bexar County Medical Center, which had decided to 'upgrade the ICU staff'. The hospital did not want the headache of the long, protracted investigation so all of the LVNs were removed from work in the ICU. All these staff members were the casualties of the hospital's reluctance for a large-scale investigation. Jones and the others were all offered jobs in other parts of the hospital and given good recommendations, but Jones resigned from the hospital on 17 March 1982.

Jones was hired almost immediately at a Kerrville-area paediatrics clinic. Dr Kathleen Holland, who had worked with Jones at the hospital while she was a resident doctor, wanted the LVN to be her right-hand woman at the new clinic. Jones and her know-it-all, dramatic personality had never bothered Dr Holland. It didn't matter to Dr Holland that Jones wasn't a registered nurse or that there were so many rumours and accusations flying around about Jones and her involvement in the baby deaths at the hospital.

One of Dr Holland's friends, another resident at the county hospital, had kindly suggested that she shouldn't hire Jones. But the hospital had offered Jones a job in another area and she had good recommendations regarding her work. Surely, if Jones was really harming children in the ICU then the hospital would have got rid of her?

So with great enthusiasm and hope for a fresh start, Jones began work at the new paediatric clinic. But the same pattern emerged. Children unexpectedly went into respiratory distress.

The emergencies coming from the new paediatrician's office in Kerrville raised concerns. Since Dr Holland's clinic had opened, the local Sid Peterson Hospital had seen more paediatric cardiac arrests than ever before. Something – or someone – was not right. Children who were presenting for normal doctor visits for the treatment of colds or flu symptoms were ending up in emergency medical situations.

Jones continued her grandiose behaviour when the children were transferred to Sid Peterson Hospital from Dr Holland's office. Jones would upset hospital staff with her condescending attitude and need to display her perceived superior nursing knowledge. It was always a drama when Genene Jones was around. *Always.*

Chelsea McClellan, 15 months old, went for a check-up at Dr Holland's clinic on 17 September 1982. Chelsea had visited the clinic before, on 24 August. It had been a dramatic introduction to the new clinic. Mrs McClellan said she had made the August appointment for Chelsea because the infant had a bad cold. While she was giving Dr Holland Chelsea's medical history, Jones (at the nurse's suggestion) had taken the little girl to another part of the clinic under the guise of giving the doctor and mother some privacy. Minutes later, Jones summoned Dr Holland because Chelsea had a seizure and had stopped breathing. Chelsea was rushed to Sid Peterson Hospital and spent more than a week there; however, doctors could not find the cause of the seizures and respiratory arrest. Mrs McClellan was baffled, but was grateful to Dr Holland and Genene Jones because she was convinced they had saved her daughter's life. The incident did not deter Mrs McClellan from using Dr Holland's services again.

Less than a month later, on that fateful September day, Genene Jones told Mrs McClellan she would update Chelsea's shots and took the mother and daughter into an examination room. According to Mrs McClellan, she hadn't even planned on taking Chelsea to the clinic but when she'd rung about an appointment for her older son, the clinic receptionist told her Dr Holland wanted to check on the little girl who just weeks before had nearly died.

In the examination room, Mrs McClellan held Chelsea, who was facing her mother, as Jones gave the infant the first shot in her left thigh. The little's girl's breathing became troubled almost immediately after the injection. Chelsea was struggling to cry out 'Mama' but the words wouldn't come. Mrs McClellan could see her daughter's condition change right in front of her eyes and it was all happening so quickly she didn't have time to stop Nurse Jones from giving the little girl another injection, this time in her right leg. That's when baby Chelsea stopped breathing and Jones yelled at the startled young mother to get the doctor.

Recalling the nightmare incident to *ABC News* in 2013, when news of Jones's possible parole was reported by the media, Mrs McClellan said, 'Genene had this wild look in her eyes, like she was on a high. She got really excited, and she yelled that Chelsea was not breathing. She grabbed her from me and put her on a table. She told me to go get the doctor.'

Chelsea's breathing had stabilised by the time the ambulance arrived and it was decided the little girl would be transferred to hospital. Jones insisted she would ride in the ambulance with her little patient. Mrs McClellan followed in her car. But during that ambulance ride, Jones gave Chelsea another injection of succinylcholine chloride, a powerful muscle relaxant. Chelsea died in the ambulance.

In October 1982, a Kerr County grand jury opened hearings on the unexplained illnesses of children at the Kerrville clinic. In May 1983, the grand jury had heard enough evidence to indict Jones for the murder of 15-month-old Chelsea McClellan. Little Chelsea's body had been exhumed on 7 May and her tissue samples were sent to Sweden to be examined by Dr Bo Holmstedt. Dr Holmstedt was the only doctor in the world at the time who had been able to test for the presence of the muscle relaxant drug succinylcholine in embalmed tissue. The test took a few weeks and District Attorney Sutton was sent the results, which showed that the drug was found in Chelsea's body. On 25 May a pair of Texas rangers arrested Jones.

Kerr County District Attorney Ronald Sutton said the nine-month investigation was hampered by the unusual nature of the alleged incidents.

'You try to understand why someone would try to injure a child,' Mr Sutton said. 'You don't expect to find that in a medical environment.'

There was also a grand jury hearing on the San Antonio hospital deaths with Bexar County District Attorney Sam Millsap leading the investigations. Eventually, after 10 months of investigations and witness testimonies, the San Antonio grand jury was able to indict Jones on charges of causing serious injury to four-week-old Rolando Santos on 9 January 1982. Jones was accused of injecting baby Rolando with heparin, an anti-coagulant drug that can cause excessive bleeding.

Peter Elkind published the first comprehensive account of the whole case in his best-selling book *The Death Shift*, released in 1984. His original feature article, also called 'The Death Shift' that became the genesis for the book was published in *Texas Monthly* in August 1983. Elkind met with Jones in May 1983 – a few weeks before she was indicted for the murder of a Chelsea McClellan. At the time, Jones was 33 and living in a mobile home with her 19-year-old husband, whom she had married a month prior.

'I'm sick and tired of being crucified alive and having people think I'm a baby killer,' she told Elkind. 'I haven't killed a damn soul.'

Jones told Elkind the baby deaths were the fault of doctors.

'I've been in nursing since 1977, and Bexar County's the only place I've been killing people?' she furiously told Elkind, who published her comments in his feature article. 'If you're going to sit there and say that I killed babies, you're going to have to tell me that a doctor ordered me to do it,' she said.

Genene Jones's trial began in January 1984.

Chelsea McClellan's mother Petti gave heartbreaking testimony about the day her baby girl died.

Mrs McClellan said Chelsea 'went limp, like a rag doll, just like a rag doll – she looked like Raggedy Ann'.

'She wasn't breathing right,' Mrs McClellan said. 'Her eyes – she was looking at me, whimpering and trying to say "Mama", but she couldn't get it out.'

Dr Holland, who was facing several negligence suits from parents of children who had suffered injury while being treated at her clinic, gave details of every child treated when the series of unexplained seizures occurred.

As she detailed each incident, District Attorney Ronald Sutton wrote them on a chart visible to the court. The chart showed that every patient under two years old that was given an intravenous (IV) injection prepared by Jones had stopped breathing and had to be resuscitated.

'Every time an IV prepared by Jones was used, a child went down, is that correct?' Mr Sutton asked.

'Yes,' Dr Holland replied.

It was suggested by some witnesses that Jones wanted to prove there was a need for a paediatric intensive care unit at the Sid Peterson Hospital. A nursing school classmate Mary Morris told the court that Jones told her the reason she moved to work with Dr Holland was to help start a specialist ICU for sick children in the area.

Ms Morris recalled telling Jones, 'We have sick children, but I don't think there's enough to fill a children's special care wing.'

Ms Morris testified that Jones replied, 'Oh, they're out there. All you have to do is go find them.'

On 16 February 1984, the seven-woman, five-man jury took an hour to find Jones guilty of murder. Jones was stunned at the verdict. She was sentenced to 99 years, with a 20-year minimum to be served before she could be eligible for parole.

One of the jurors Anne Bradley said she felt that Jones was very dangerous.

'She can fit into our medical institutions and so smoothly accomplish those deeds,' Ms Bradley told the Associated Press.

Chelsea's parents, Petti and Reid, addressed the media outside the courtroom after the verdict. Crying while thanking the jurors, Mrs McClellan described the time since her baby's death as a 'twilight zone'.

'For a long time I thought it was my fault, like I shouldn't have taken her to that doctor's office,' Mrs McClellan said. 'It put a strain on our marriage. I feel like now we can really tell Chelsea goodbye and we can get on with our lives.'

Jones faced another trial in October 1984 for the charges that she deliberately injured four-week-old Rolando Santos in San Antonio while working at the Bexar County hospital. Rolando survived but the medical emergency was extremely distressing for the baby and his family.

The evidence was damning against Jones, but investigators were not able to bring murder charges against her for the unexpected deaths of the babies at the hospital ICU even though they *knew* she was involved. There was *no other* explanation.

An expert in the study of disease populations gave testimony about a study he conducted into the incidences of resuscitation in the ICU between 1981 and 1982. Dr Greg Istre, the Oklahoma State Epidemiologist, told the court that this timeframe was considered an 'epidemic' of events. Dr Istre's study found that infants in the ICU experienced cardiac arrest more than 10 times higher during the time that Genene Jones was on shift. Wire service United Press International reported from the court that Dr Istre said during the timeframe he studied, nine children required multiple cardiopulmonary resuscitations and Jones was assigned to all but one of those patients.

Nurse Suzanna Maldonado also gave testimony about being sent a death threat at the time she had expressed concern to her supervisor about the deaths of the babies in the ICU. Ms Maldonado said Genene Jones had written a note on her nursing assignment sheet for 16 March 1982 that read: 'check your [mail]box'. Ms Maldonado told the court that when she did check her mailbox 'there was a piece of paper in it that said "your [sic] dead"'.

On 24 October 1984, Jones was convicted of injuring baby Roland with an injection of heparin and sentenced to 60 years' jail, to be served concurrently with her life sentence.

In an embarrassing and worrying administrative oversight, a letter was sent from the Texas Department of Corrections to the Bexar County Hospital district board asking if Jones was qualified to work in a prison hospital dispensary. The letter was leaked to the media in November 1984, and Associated Press reported that Dr William Thornton, the hospital board chairman, forwarded the letter immediately to District Attorney Sam Millsap.

Mr Millsap told Associated Press that he never heard from the Texas Board of Corrections again.

'Had they [prison representatives] called me I would have told them that under no circumstances would I recommend that she [Jones] be allowed near a hospital, let alone a prison hospital,' Mr Millsap said.

It is believed that the letter was routine and for the purposes of determining how prisoners could use their skills while incarcerated.

Despite her 99-year sentence, Jones first became eligible for parole in November 1988 but it didn't mean she would be released. The public was dismayed that the baby killer could even be considered for parole and the Texas State Board of Pardons received almost 600 letters of protest after the matter was publicised on the high-rating daytime talk show at the time *Geraldo*.

Ron Sutton, who by then was the district attorney, and who prosecuted the case back in 1984, said he would protest the parole.

'She has never admitted her guilt in this thing. For that reason I consider her extremely dangerous,' Mr Sutton told the Associated Press.

In 1991, a television movie called *Deadly Medicine* told the story of the events that occurred at Dr Holland's paediatric clinic. Popular television actress Veronica Hamel (from *Hill Street Blues*) played Dr Holland and Susan Ruttan, best known at the time for playing Roxanne Melman on *L.A. Law*, portrayed Jones. Dr Holland served as a consultant on the film and was still trying to reclaim hospital privileges that were revoked almost a decade before.

In 1992, the *Kerrville Daily Times* reported that parole officials were re-examining Jones's case. The parents of Chelsea McClellan were outraged at the prospect. Petti McClellan told the newspaper she was furious.

'I would just die if she got out,' she said. 'She'll do it again. I'm just as sure of that as I am sure of my name.'

Mr Sutton added, 'I consider her to be one of the most dangerous people in the United States … the most sensational child killer in the US.'

A Texas Law at the time of Jones's conviction means that she could have gone free from prison as early as May 2018. The Mandatory Release

Law was designed to relieve prison overcrowding and allows prisoners convicted of violent crimes between 1977 and 1987 to be automatically released with good behaviour 'credits' and time already served. The law was changed to exclude violent criminals but has not been applied retroactively to prisoners like Jones.

Speaking on *Raising America* on the HLN cable TV network, Bexar County Criminal District Attorney Susan D Reed said she was looking at building a case to try to block Jones's parole.

'She was implicated in the deaths of 47 little babies and my goodness, we cannot have someone like that free. Period,' Ms Reed told host Kyra Phillips in April 2013.

'She should never walk out of prison. It is an automatic parole under the law at the time of her conviction so there's nothing I can do about that ... I understand there is the possibility of a compassionate parole based on a medical condition and I'm certainly going to protest that because anybody who shows so little compassion for children should not receive compassion under the parole system.'

Sam Millsap, the Bexar County District Attorney who investigated Jones for the hospital deaths, said a new case had to be made against the deadly nurse to make sure she could never be freed. Mr Millsap recounted the difficulties of the initial investigation to television host Kyra Phillips.

'We had both practical and political obstacles that we had to deal with at the time. Murder investigations begin with committed complainants and in this case we started out with nothing more than a tip. In addition is that in a criminal case you have to prove guilt beyond a reasonable doubt,' Mr Millsap said via live interview.

'The passage of time is the enemy of a prosecutor. Cases typically don't get better, they deteriorate over time. Witnesses die, witnesses move, records are lost. Thirty years have passed. The people who tried to impede our investigation 30 years ago are no longer around...'

Joyce Riley, a former nurse, broke her decades of silence and also spoke to *Raising America* about her time working with Genene Jones. Ms Riley had audited records at the county hospital and said she found the link between the infant deaths and the 3pm to 11pm shift that Jones worked.

'I was told "I'm sorry Joyce, but if you say that again you'll be fired, sued for slander and you'll never work again",' Ms Riley recalled in the 2013 interview.

Ms Riley was moved on from her position while Jones stayed in the ICU.

'Imagine a child laying [sic] there, not knowing that this woman was playing with him like a cat plays with a mouse … she would find some way … that she would crash that baby and knowing how she crashed that baby she could help revive the baby and be the hero. She loved that,' Ms Riley said.

Ms Riley said Chelsea McClellan should never have died and hospital administrators had a lot to answer for. She said she wished she had confronted Jones at the time and she deeply regretted not doing so.

There is now a push to find other parents whose babies Jones might have killed and who are willing to have their children's deaths investigated.

A Facebook group was set up for people who believe their loved ones were victims of Jones. The page, called 'Victims of Genene Anne Jones' has more than 800 members that include families whose children died at the time Jones worked at Bexar County Hospital and the Kerrville clinic, private investigators, journalists and others who have taken an interest.

One of the group's members, Annie Kadilis says Genene Jones murdered her baby sister.

Annie was just six when her three-month-old baby sister Placida died. Baby Placida died at the Bexar County Hospital in October 1981. She was born with an enlarged heart and her short life was spent in and out of hospitals. Annie said she doesn't remember much about baby Placida but does have a cherished memory of being at their grandmother's house.

'I was kneeling down on the floor next to where she lay and she had her cute little chubby baby fingers wrapped around my finger,' Annie said via email.

A mother of three children aged 19, 17 and three, Annie has lived with the tragedy of her sister's murder. Annie explained that in 1985 her parents received a settlement from the hospital and signed a contract, which stipulated they were never to speak to the media. For this reason, her parents will not be named here.

'I signed no such contract because well, I was about six when everything happened ...so all I can do is tell you what I can recall,' Annie wrote. Her story follows:

Placida got sick and had to go into the hospital. She was in the hospital for a few days and was doing very well. She was almost ready to come home. My parents were there with her, 24/7. Genene Jones was Placida's nurse the day that she died. My parents were sitting in the room with my sister when Genene Jones went into my sister's room. I was not there so I can only tell you what I've heard throughout the years and the story has never changed. She [Jones] leaned over my sister, my mom couldn't see what she was doing to my sister, then the monitor started beeping and she yelled at my parents to leave the room. The next time my parents saw my sister, she was dead...

Annie said her parents were only told in 1985 that Jones had killed their baby. While they received a sum of money at the time as part of a private hospital settlement, Annie said her mother 'climbed into the bottom of a beer bottle' for a decade after Placida's death. 'But my mother is a wonderful, strong woman,' Annie added.

Annie became a surrogate mother to her little brother while her parents were headlong into their grief and, in her words 'emotionally unavailable'. The tragedy has also cast a shadow over her own parenting experiences:

I tend to cling to my children and I'm so damn overprotective that sometimes I annoy myself LOL ['laugh out loud']. It's like I see monsters around every corner. I have severe trust issues, not just with medical professionals but also with everyone. This past January my three-year-old had a burst appendix and had to have an operation. He was in the hospital for eight days and for the entire time we were there I was suspicious of every poor nurse that went into his room. Every medical procedure any of my children have had to have over the past 19 years has given me panic attacks...

Unless a case can be made to try Jones for the murders of more babies, she will be released from prison.

In August 2014, Jones was denied parole with the Texas Board of Pardons and Parole giving her a 'serve all' notice, which means she must serve the entirety of her sentence.

That gives Susan Reed, victims' advocate Andy Kahan and others a few more years to find new leads on other killings committed by Jones.

'It would be a tragedy to let this woman out of jail,' Annie said. 'She should have been given a death sentence and executed years ago.'

In April 2018 *Texas Monthly* revealed that Jones had confessed in a 1998 prison interview ahead of a parole hearing, allegedly saying, 'I really did kill those babies'. In the article by Peter Elkind, who wrote the book *The Death Shift* about Jones, it was also reported that a fellow inmate of Jones wrote to the parole board alleging the killer nurse admitted to her: 'I didn't kill those babies. The voices in my head did.'

Jones appeared again in court in February 2019 and was declared competent to stand trial on five new charges of baby murders, to which she pleaded not guilty. Her lawyer Cornelius Cox requested another psychiatric evaluation, which was granted by the judge Andrew Carruthers. On 22 May 2019 Jones's lawyer appeared in court to request the return of some of the killer nurse's personal belongings, including a Bible, which had handwritten notes. This request was denied, with the Judge for this hearing, Frank Castro ruling in favour of the prosecution team's assertions that items, especially her Bible showed Jones's ability to read, write and comprehend the new criminal proceedings against her.

Assistant District Attorney Catherine Babbitt told news crews outside the court: 'The Bible contains some handwriting, I'm not going to get in the specifics of that, but that may or may not be relevant down the road'.

At the time of writing, a competency hearing was expected to occur in August or September 2019.

Lainz Death Angels

- A Hospital Killing Team -

Work chatter over drinks at a wine bar was the catalyst for the discovery of one of the worst crimes in Austria's history.

In February 1989, four nurse's aides from Lainz Hospital were relaxing in a local pub after a hard day and swapping work stories. But these work stories and jokes involved laughing about a patient who had recently died. Dark humour is not uncommon among medical staff, but these women were bragging and joking about the death because *they had caused it*. Unbeknownst to the women, a doctor was nearby and overheard the conversation. Horrified, he went to the police with what he had heard and an investigation began.

Built in 1839 in Lainz, a southwest suburb of Vienna, Lainz General Hospital was the fourth-largest medical facility in Austria, with mre than 1000 beds. Pavilion V was a last stop for elderly patients who had no family or friends to care for them in their final months.

Rumours of strange deaths had been circulating around at the hospital for several years already. In April 1988, one nurse mentioned to other staff members that there was talk that patients were being 'put to rest' by a group of nurses. The rumours persisted and senior medical colleagues at the hospital started to hear about the disturbing tales of the 'mercy' killings of patients in their care. But who would really believe that a gang of the hospital's nurses would be taking the lives of the sick and vulnerable? Certainly not many people who heard the rumours took the tales seriously. One nurse reported her concerns to a doctor about a suspicious death in 1988 of an elderly female patient, who had died of an apparent sleeping pill overdose. These concerns were relayed to police, but subsequent inquiries did not reveal any wrongdoing. However, it would later be revealed that a wall of silence greeted detectives who tried to investigate the rumours.

On 7 April 1989, police arrested nurse's aides Waltraud Wagner, 30, Maria Gruber, 25, Irene Leidolf, 27, and Stephanija Mayer, 50. Suspicions of the deliberate insulin overdoses of two patients had been raised on 5 April. One of the patients had died and the other had recovered. Just days after the arrests, the women confessed to almost 50 killings.

With the exception of Mayer, all the women were from small towns in Austria and had relocated to the bustle of Vienna. Mayer was from Yugoslavia.

On 11 April 1989, Police Chief Guenter Boegl told a news conference on the murders, 'We do not yet know where it will end'. Mr Boegl said the women chose victims they considered hopeless and too sick and injected them with sedatives. Most of the victims were aged between 75 to 80 years. In many cases, the women claimed, the patients had begged for them to end their lives. There was also another method the women used: the water cure, which involved forcing water into the lungs of the victim, who would then suffocate and drown. This was done under the guise of performing 'oral hygiene care', which was for the care of people in comas and was only supposed to be carried out by nurses.

While all the women killed patients, it became apparent that Waltraud Wagner was the leader of the group.

Waltraud Wagner had worked at Lainz Hospital since 1975. She became fascinated with death after witnessing a doctor give the sedative Rohypnol to an elderly patient who then almost died. It did something to the tired, overworked Wagner. She saw the power of life and death that doctors and nurses could wield.

At her trial, Wagner was described by the prosecution as the sadistic leader of the gang, instructing the others on the proper techniques of lethal injection and the 'water cure'. Moving from 'compassion' to sadism, the women began killing patients who annoyed them – snoring, soiling the bed, refusing medication, or asking for help too often were reasons to be issued a 'ticket to God'.

Wagner was charged with the most murders – 32 counts as well as two attempted killings. She was given the names of patients who had died on her ward in recent years and she checked off the names of 39 people she said she had killed.

Max Edelbacher, head of Vienna Police's Criminal Division, told the enthralled media that he 'got the subjective impression that the doctors could have been more strict in their supervision'. (Edelbacher was later involved in the hunt for Austrian kidnapping victim Natascha Kampusch, who went missing in 1998 at age 10. Ms Kampusch escaped from her captor eight years later in 2006.) The investigation had uncovered a disturbing picture of dangerous work practices under the strain of an overburdened health system. Edelbacher said that upon questioning hospital staff, police found that there was a decent amount of 'knowledge and suspicion' about the deaths and that senior personnel did not seem to take these rumours seriously.

Dr Franz Pesendorfer, who was in charge of the ward, was suspended by the head of the hospital because of his reported refusal to cooperate with authorities during the 1988 investigation. The doctor was heavily criticised by Austria's press with newspaper *Neue Kronen Zeitung* writing an editorial that asserted that the lack of action by hospital doctors when they were first alerted to rumours meant that the murderous gang killed an extra 22 people between April 1988 and April 1989. One of those victims was a former prima ballerina of the famous Vienna State Opera, Julia Drapal. During the women's trial in 1991, more details of the killings were revealed including Ms Drapal's. Irene Leidolf admitted she gave the woman an overdose of a tranquiliser 'to free her from her pain and make it easier for her to die'.

The women arrested were aides, which meant their role was to wash and feed patients and provide support to qualified nurses who administered medication and injections. However, the gang was running rampant, making judgments on who should live and who should die. The investigation into the killings revealed that lesser-qualified staff could access medications, including insulin, which was against hospital policy.

The 'Death Angels of Lainz' caused the most criminal atrocities in Austria's history since World War II. The women and their shocking crimes were likened to the death angels of Auschwitz. The crimes brought back painful memories for many Austrians. In 1938 most of the country supported *Anschluss*, which was the union of Austria and Germany. The far-right pro-Nazi Party in Austria had grown during the 1930s, which made it easy for Austrian-born Adolf Hitler to combine the nations, as had been a dream of his since he was a young man. At the time of *Anschluss*, Austria had a Jewish population of around 200,000. Many of these Jews fled as it became apparent that Austria had become a nameless state consumed by Germany, where they had begun to be persecuted. Mobs rampaged through villages and towns, ripping down Austrian flags and replacing them with those of the Nazi Party, which bore the infamous swastika. Around 60,000 Jewish people were unable to leave and were sent to concentration camps, as well as around 10,000 Roma and other ethnic minorities, political opponents and Catholics.

In a 1989 interview with *Chicago Tribune*, Professor Erwin Ringel, a renowned psychologist and author of the best-selling book *Austrian Soul*, said the Nazi past of Austria and its effect on the nation's psyche was a reason why the women were able to kill so prolifically and went undetected for so long.

'I am convinced we were not able to overcome the feelings of the Nazi times because we have avoided facing it,' Professor Ringel said. 'We are still like the people in the Nazi times. Austrians are not willing to face the truth. The majority are driven to suppression and denial.'

A packed courtroom heard state prosecutor Ernst Kloyber describe Wagner as a woman who became 'mistress over life and death'. The other three women were in the thrall of Wagner and the killing team was feared to have killed many hundreds more vulnerable patients over six years. Associated Press reported that Wagner looked down and shook her head as Mr Kloyber outlined the prosecution's case. By this stage, the women had all retracted their initial confessions. Wagner, who said police had pressured her during the confession, now claimed she had only killed 10 people and these were only to relieve their suffering.

Mr Kloyber dismissed the women's stories that the killings were a merciful release for the already desperately ill and dying patients. He stated in court, 'It is only a small step from the murder of the incurably ill to the murder of those who appear to be incurably sick and from there to the murder of bothersome, cheeky patients.'

'Some [patients] lay for weeks, unable to die,' Wagner testified in court on 28 February 1991. 'Afterwards, I thought I'd helped them.'

Wagner told Judge Peter Straub that patients were quieter after she gave them two to three ampoules of Rohypnol.

'And what then?' the judge asked Wagner.

'Afterwards, they died,' she replied.

Wagner was visibly distressed after she stepped down from the stand, having been questioned for two hours.

Irene Leidolf, charged with four murders, burst into tears after she answered queries in court. Mayer, accused of 12 murders, was also very emotional on the stand.

As a nurse's aide, Wagner should not have had any access to medications but she readily admitted that during the night shift she could get as many sedatives she wanted from an unlocked cabinet.

The case brought to light serious – and deadly – shortfalls in hospital care in Austria. For the small nation of around eight million people, the revelations were a shock. The conditions at Lainz Hospital meant that nurse's aides such as Wagner and the others were performing tasks they simply were not qualified for or legally allowed to undertake.

The doctors and nurses were overworked too. Records were not checked properly and because the patients were elderly and infirm, it was no surprise when they died. This lax culture, driven by lack of resources and an overwhelming workload, meant that the four women could do what they wanted.

Former Lainz Hospital ward nurse Helene Speiser gave evidence at the trial that there was no reason to suspect anything amiss because Waltraud Wagner, in particular, was a good worker and well liked by her peers.

An audit of drugs revealed that on the first level of Pavilion V, where Wagner and the others worked, 2495 ampoules of Rohypnol were used on patients, as opposed to just 285 on the second level. Also, a register of deaths on the ward found that patients were up to six times more likely to die when Wagner was on duty, and when she went on leave, that number dropped starkly.

'Besides, if a patient is bad today and dead tomorrow, what is the notice? They would have died anyway,' Ms Speiser told the court.

Mr Kloyber told the eight-person jury that euthanasia was unacceptable in society.

'Society glorifies what is young, dynamic, innovative and healthy,' Mr Kloyber said. 'The old are forced to the edge of society by a dictatorship of the healthy.'

Wagner's defence counsel Wilhelm Philip said his client wanted to help the people she stood accused of murdering.

'Waltraud Wagner wanted to help, help and nothing but help,' Mr Philip told the court.

The jury deliberated for 17 hours before delivering the verdicts. The whole country was waiting on the decision. Wagner was convicted of 15 counts of murder and 17 attempted murders. She collapsed as the verdict was read. Irene Leidolf was convicted of five murders; Maria Gruber of two counts of attempted murder; and Stephanija Mayer of seven counts of attempted murder and one of manslaughter. Wagner and Leidolf were sentenced to life imprisonment, which meant they would be eligible for release after 15 years. Under Austrian law, sentences are served concurrently and not consecutively.

The women represent an exclusive group – an all-female killing team that is, to date, the most prolific in history. The true number of deaths caused by the 'Death Angels of Lainz' is believed to be as high as 300.

Authorities released Maria Gruber and Stephanija Mayer quietly sometime in the early 2000s. The women were given new identities as a precaution against vigilantes.

In 2006, it was revealed in top-selling magazine *News* that Wagner and Leidolf had been able to leave prison and go on shopping outings and to get their hair done as part of a pre-release program. Leidolf spoke with *News* from behind bars. The convicted killer told the magazine that she had a job in the prison and tended to her daily chores like washing, cooking and cleaning her cell. Leidolf also shared that she enjoyed her 'day trips' where, accompanied by prison guards, she visited boutiques, the hairdresser and her family where she could sit with them on the couch and 'eat cake'. Leidolf also said the outside world had changed much since she was jailed – '… there are so many subways… many high-rise buildings…'

In 2008, news emerged that Wagner, now 49, and Leidolf, 46, would be released after serving almost 20 years. Leidolf and Wagner are now living under new identities.

Lainz Hospital was renamed Hietzing Hospital to try to disassociate from its murderous past.

Ahmad Alami

- Horror on the Children's Ward -

A hospital is a place to feel protected and cared for but more than 40 years ago, one in England was the scene of an inconceivable crime. It is hard to believe the violent tragedy that happened and the fact that it was all caused by untreated and serious mental illness. In this case, the perpetrator was sick and no one could have predicted what followed.

Victoria Hospital in Blackpool has one of the busiest emergency departments in England and is the main hospital for residents in Lancashire in the north-west.

On Thursday, 17 February 1972, staff on the Children's Ward of the hospital were met with a horror scene. A knife-wielding assailant had seriously wounded nurse Dorothy Simpson, 49, and student nurse Christine Nuttall, 22.

The women were working on their early morning shift when a man wandered into the reception area of the ward, telling Sister Simpson that he was a staff member and was looking for some sleeping tablets. The man looked respectable enough – he was dressed smartly in a dark blue suit. However, Sister Simpson followed hospital protocol and asked to see some identification. He seemed agitated and terse. Suddenly and without warning, the man lunged and stabbed Nurse Simpson in the chest. Student nurse Nuttall tried to stop the man entering the ward but she was slashed too.

As if the senseless attack on the nurses wasn't enough, the man ran into one of the ward's rooms and started wildly stabbing at the child patients through their bedclothes as they slept in their cots. Three children were stabbed to death – Deborah Carson, four, and Martin Langhorne and Nicholas Scott, both just two years old. Another toddler, Darren Qamar, also two, was critically injured but saved by surgeons. Little Darren suffered injuries to his vertebrae, spleen and liver. In an even more tragic twist, Darren's mother was attending her mother's funeral in Ireland on the day her little boy was stabbed.

A dangerous madman was on the loose in the hospital grounds. If he had attacked little children, God only knew what else he was capable of.

Roadblocks around the hospital were hurriedly put in place and every available police officer in Blackpool was brought in to hunt for the brutal killer. Police warned that the killer could be a drug addict who could strike again and put other hospitals and pharmacies on high alert.

But the danger had come from within. It didn't take the police long to find the killer from the description given by the nurses and other witnesses. A Jordanian-born doctor was the culprit. Dr Ahmed Alami, 32, was an eye specialist and a resident at the hospital.

Lancashire Police Chief Constable William Palfrey said, 'This is one of the worst murders with which I have been involved during my 45 years of police service.'

The father of Deborah Carson told reporters his little girl had been treated for bronchitis in the hospital and was due to come home the day after she was murdered. 'I just don't understand it. Why? Why?' Mr Carson asked.

The Blackpool community had already faced a tragedy in the preceding year when police superintendent Gerald Richardson was killed on 23 August 1971 when he attended an armed hold-up at a jewellery store. A store clerk pressed an alarm during the hold-up that brought police to the scene. A gang of five men blasted their way out of the store with sawn-off shotguns and Superintendent Richardson was fatally wounded. The man who shot the policeman was on the run for 45 days until he was arrested in a dawn raid on a bedsit in North London on 8 October 1971.

Frederick Joseph Sewell, a South London used-car dealer, was the most wanted man in Britain at the time of his arrest and he was subsequently sentenced to life imprisonment.

Such was the public outrage over the Victoria Hospital murders that Alami wore a blanket over his head as he was led to court for a charge hearing that lasted just three minutes.

Alami had lived in Britain for two years and came from one of the highest profile families in Jordan. His father was the highest Muslim religious leader in Jerusalem, Sheikh Saad Eddin Alami.

Known as the Mufti of Jerusalem, he was reported to have burst into tears when told of his son's actions. (The Mufti later helped establish and became the Head of the Supreme Islamic Council, the highest religious body for East Jerusalem and the Occupied West Bank. He died in 1993, aged 82.) Alami's sister Dalal, who lived in the Jordanian capital Amman, told a United Press International (UPI) reporter that her brother was 'subject to nervous breakdowns' and had moved to England in 1970. UPI reported she said her brother was usually 'a man who hates violence, who is extremely kind to children'.

Alami had worked at the world-famous Moorfields Eye Hospital in London before taking employment at Blackpool Victoria Hospital as a senior house officer (someone who is in their second year of hospital work after graduating medical school) in the ophthalmic department. Before then, Alami had worked at a hospital in Bournemouth, Dorset. Here, his behaviour had raised such serious concerns among staff that he was seen by psychiatrists, which resulted in a diagnosis of paranoid schizophrenia.

In fact, Alami's fragile mental condition had emerged in the 1960s when he was in Jordan and worked in the army medical corps. He was forced to resign from the army and he then travelled to Britain. None of this was known to the London hospitals he worked at and due to patient confidentiality, none of his employers were notified of his new diagnosis of paranoid schizophrenia. He was being treated with tranquilisers and a few months before the murders he visited his psychiatrist again, who advised him to keep taking the medication. Alami was married but his wife had returned to Jordan in the months before the murders.

At Lancaster Crown Court the selected jury decided that Alami was not fit to plead to the charges. The jury was told during preliminary hearings that Victoria Hospital had not been aware of Alami's psychiatric history and diagnosis as a paranoid schizophrenic.

He was sent to Broadmoor Hospital, a high security facility in Berkshire, England that has housed Britain's most dangerous killers.

Not much more was heard of Dr Alami. He was quietly released in 1976 and returned to Bethlehem where he received more psychiatric treatment and was under the watch of his father, who was still the Mufti of the ancient city.

Alami never worked as a doctor again but became a historian and has written 25 books on Palestinian history.

Alami's name resurfaced again in British newspapers when he applied in 1997 for a visa to live and study in the country for a PhD in political science. His application was rejected but Alami appealed the decision. Under British immigration law, a Home Office review tribunal could consider the application again.

Mary Qamar, mother of Darren Qamar, who was critically injured in the attack, was appalled when she found out about Alami's bid to return to England.

'The man has a damned cheek. He should never be allowed back ever. I still feel very bitter, and so does Darren who is still suffering from his injuries after all these years,' Mrs Qamar told her local paper the *Luton News* in 2000, when they rang and told her about Alami's visa appeal.

'He suffered injuries to his vertebrae, spleen and liver. He was ripped to pieces internally. He had plastic surgery but it wasn't very successful. He was permanently scarred and is still suffering today… the only good thing was that the knife missed his face,' Mrs Qamar told the newspaper.

'Never a day goes by without me thinking about it and those poor children who were killed, and their families,' she said.

The *Luton News* reprinted the words of Alami, who was approached for comment by a national Sunday newspaper, in a 2 February 2000 edition.

> *I have wanted to write to the families of those children I killed and apologise to them, but I was advised that it was best not to reawaken those emotions. I am now cured. I wished to come back to Britain unnoticed. Now that you [the newspapers] know, it is possible I will be confronted by the father of one of the children I killed.*

Kristen Gilbert

- Cold-hearted Killer -

Something wasn't right at the Veterans Affairs Medical Center in Northampton, Massachusetts.

Between 12 October 1995 and 21 February 1996 a series of unusual deaths and medical incidents raised concerns among the medical personnel.

While the federally run and funded hospital treated some extremely vulnerable and complex medical cases of veterans, many of whom were elderly, patients were dying from heart failure that was completely unrelated to their other health conditions. In fact, the number of cardiac arrests increased to the point that several nurses came forward to report their fears that there was a killer among them.

One case that stood out in particular was that of 35-year-old air force veteran Henry Hudon, who had schizophrenia and was a frequent patient at the hospital to have his medications adjusted.

On 8 December 1995, Mr Hudon was admitted to the Veteran Affairs (VA) Medical Center with flu symptoms. He died six days later of an apparent heart attack. Mr Hudon's sister Christine Duquette was adamant her brother had never had any heart problems and she was convinced he met with foul play. An autopsy revealed he had died of poisoning from epinephrine (also known as adrenaline), which can overstimulate the heart. This drug can be a lifesaver when someone has heart failure, but if given to someone with a normally functioning heart can cause cardiac arrest.

Staff also noticed that vials of epinephrine were regularly going missing.

Another patient Kenneth Cutting, 41, went into cardiac arrest and died at the hospital on 2 February 1996. Mr Cutting had multiple sclerosis and was blind but his widow Nancy Cutting said he had never had any known issues with his heart.

Mrs Cutting was understandably distraught when she was told that her husband had died, but thought it must have been 'by the grace of God' after the health battles he had endured.

However, there was something far, far from God's will happening at that hospital.

By all appearances, Kristen Gilbert was a popular, competent registered nurse and an attractive, fun-loving woman. She graduated from nursing school in 1988 and began her career at the VA hospital in 1989, when she was a newlywed and living in the town with her husband Glenn. By the age of 26, Gilbert was the mother of two sons and continued to work at the hospital, swapping from the day shift to the 4pm-to-midnight shift on Ward C, which was an intensive care unit.

At work, Gilbert struck up a friendship with James Perrault, a member of the hospital security, who was also a Gulf War veteran. Whenever there was an emergency call at the hospital, Perrault would rush to respond. The pair flirted and spent time after their shifts having some drinks at a nearby bar frequented by hospital staff. They began an affair, with Gilbert telling her new lover that her seven-year marriage was on the rocks anyway.

It is thought that Gilbert actually tried to kill her husband. She was never indicted for the attempted murder of Glenn Gilbert but prosecutors were well aware of what happened and had spoken at length to him about the attempts on his life.

On 5 November 1995, Glenn Gilbert was hospitalised with severe gastroenteritis and blood tests found that he had unusually low levels of potassium and glucose. From Mr Gilbert's recollections, the government prosecutors believed this was a result of Gilbert lacing her husband's food with diuretics over a period of several weeks. One of the side effects of this was that his heart was beating irregularly. When her husband was discharged, Gilbert openly complained that a follow-up potassium test was not done. This led the way for her to make the alleged attempt on his life.

Mr Gilbert later testified that Gilbert brought home two syringes, one pre-filled with a clear liquid, and told her husband she would take a blood sample back to the hospital so that they could test his potassium levels. Firstly, she had to flush his vein with saline and when she injected him, Mr Gilbert later recalled that his chest and arm went numb.

As he recoiled from the injection, Mr Gilbert said his wife 'pinned him against the wall with her hip' and continued. He blacked out for a brief time but regained consciousness and no other medical intervention was needed. When he expressed his confusion at the incident, Gilbert told him that he had simply fainted at the sight of the syringe. Government authorities believed Gilbert had tried to inject her husband with potassium that would have caused a fatal heart attack.

Gilbert had told Perrault that her husband was violent towards *her*. In December 1995, Gilbert left her marriage and moved into an apartment on her own.

Meanwhile, at the VA hospital, Gilbert's colleagues had noticed that ever since she had started to work the evening shift, patient deaths had increased. And Gilbert always seemed to be around when one of the veterans died unexpectedly.

Fellow nurses had seen Gilbert enter the rooms of some of the men who later died, under the pretence of flushing their intravenous lines. This would require the use of saline, a harmless, painless substance; however, there were a few men who reported feeling a burning, painful sensation in their arms when Gilbert flushed their IV lines.

There had been too many incidents now for staff to ignore. As well as their suspicions about Gilbert, there were the matters of missing vials of epinephrine that could not be accounted for and the fact that the drug was being used without authorisation. An investigation began in late February 1996. Gilbert immediately left her job and most telling, the death rate during her former shift began to drop. There were not the dramatic code events that were a hallmark of her presence on the evening shift.

Her great love affair with Perrault was now faltering. She pumped Perrault for information about the investigation but gradually, when it became obvious that Gilbert *was the focus* of the investigation, he started to withdraw. Perrault, who had aspirations of joining the police force, wondered if it was such a good idea to be entangled with Gilbert. She became bitter and isolated and thought her lover was betraying her to investigators. Gilbert's behaviour became more and more erratic – she threatened Perrault, and when he tried to end the relationship in June 1996, she became unstable and suicidal. On a number of occasions she was admitted to hospital psychiatric wards, and she also began to stalk Perrault. In the midst of a divorce from her husband Glenn, she was also unable to be a stable mother to her two sons, who were aged five and two.

By September the relationship was over and Perrault had an appointment for an interview with the investigators from the United States Attorney's Office. He told Gilbert the date and time of this interview and she begged him not to attend.

As detailed in court documents, on 26 September 1996, the day of the interview, Gilbert attempted to physically stop her ex-lover speaking to investigators by blocking his driveway with her car. Following the interview, Perrault returned to his car to find the air had been let out of his front tyre. Over the next week eggs were thrown at Perrault's car, the windshield spray-painted, the exterior was scratched with a key, and the front licence plate damaged.

During his shift at the hospital the evening of the interview, Perrault received a number of threatening calls at the security desk. The calls were dialled directly to the desk and the voice was unidentified and 'distorted'. One call said, 'There are three explosive devices in building one. You have two hours,' and another, 'This is my last call. In 25 minutes, I'll see you in hell.' As a result, 50 very ill patients were moved by wheelchairs and stretchers to another building. No suspicious or explosive devices were found.

Suspecting the caller was Gilbert, Perrault agreed to work with investigators and told his disgruntled ex when he would be back on shift at the hospital. Tellingly, no strange calls were received when Perrault was not at work. A surveillance team tracked Gilbert; her fingerprint was found on a payphone that was proved to have been used to call the hospital and a search of her home discovered a voice distorter toy and packets of batteries. Police also found the instructions to the voice distorter in the pocket of her jacket and an issue of the *Daily Hampshire Gazette*, dated 27 September 1996, with an article on the bomb threat from 26 September.

In January 1998, Kristen Gilbert was found guilty by a jury of making telephone bomb threats and sentenced to 15 months in federal prison.

During the trial, prosecutors said that Gilbert was motivated to make the calls to get back at Perrault for dumping her and to interfere with the investigation of the hospital deaths.

In November 1998, Gilbert was charged with murder and attempted murder. She maintained her innocence and was held in custody without bail.

For a *Boston Globe* feature on Gilbert, published the week before her trial began, staff writer Thomas Farragher interviewed people who worked with and grew up with the accused nurse.

'Things with Kristen weren't always the way they seemed,' said Frank Bertrand, a VA nurse. 'I don't know if she had two personalities or something that she could turn on or turn off, much like an actor playing a role.'

Others said they could not fault the nursing skills of Gilbert and said in her younger years as a nurse, she was at the hub of the staff social life.

And those who grew up with Gilbert in the suburbs of Boston recalled a girl who lied a lot. Boyfriends said she could be manipulative and her own father admitted that she was a habitual liar.

Court documents that were unsealed when Gilbert was charged with the crimes showed she had an alleged history of violence towards patients that dated back a decade.

There was an allegation from 1987 that she scalded a man with hot water when she was treating him on a home visit, and another incident in 1994 where she removed a patient's breathing tube at the VA hospital and caused a medical emergency. Another of the allegations included Gilbert forcing an untrained colleague to use cardiac defibrillation paddles on a patient during a medical emergency and refusing to help.

A 4 December 1999 Associated Press article 'Nurse reportedly has history of violence' by Trudy Tynan commented on the allegations of previous violence: 'She [Gilbert] has not been charged in the cases, but prosecutors contend they establish a pattern in which she used her position "to gain access to patients, to cause medical emergencies and deaths and to conceal those crimes".'

While Massachusetts is considered one of the more liberal states in America (the death penalty was ruled unconstitutional in 1982 and the last person to have been executed there was in 1947), the prosecutors were allowed to seek capital punishment for Gilbert. Gilbert's crimes occurred on United States Government property (the government-funded VA hospital), thereby making her eligible for the federal death penalty. In 1999 the then Attorney General Janet Reno approved the decision to seek the death penalty.

US Attorney Donald Stern outlined why Gilbert's alleged crimes were so grave and that capital punishment was an option. 'The patients were murdered in their hospital beds by a nurse who used her position and her specialised knowledge to commit the crimes,' Mr Stern said.

Jury selection for the capital murder trial was difficult. The legal teams were concerned that it would be hard to find jurors whose views of Gilbert were not tainted from knowledge of her prior trial and jail sentence for the bomb hoax to the hospital.

The Associated Press reported 800 potential jurors congregated to fill out questionnaires about their background and opinions so that the court could find 12 jurors and six alternates. It was such a big undertaking that the process was held at the Springfield Symphony Hall rather than the courthouse.

Presiding over the high-profile trial was US District Judge Michael Ponsor (now also an author of legal thriller).

Judge Ponsor ran a tight trial and was strict with what the jury was allowed to hear. In a blow to the prosecutors, Judge Ponsor barred them from using a study by University of Massachusetts Professor Stephan Gelbach that showed three-quarters of the hospital's deaths over a period of several years happened during Gilbert's shifts.

Associated Press reported on 16 October 2000 that Professor Gelbach had said in the report there was a one in one million probability that Gilbert would have been present during all those deaths simply by chance.

Gilbert gave no testimony during her trial so the jurors were reliant on the words and opinions of many medical experts as well as hospital employees.

Among the cases described, the court heard that on 21 August 1995, Stanley Jagodowski, a 66-year-old Army veteran, was heard to yell, 'Ow, ow, you're killing me!' According to the prosecution, Gilbert was seen entering Mr Jagodowski's room prior to that with a syringe. Shortly afterwards Mr Jagodowski went into cardiac arrest and the following day he died.

On 22 January 1996, Thomas Callahan, 60, went into cardiac arrest in the ICU while under Gilbert's care. He was stabilised but nurses found used epinephrine ampoules in the syringe disposal following the emergency.

The prosecution put forward that Gilbert created the emergency events, in part to get attention and also to impress her lover Mr Perrault. The code events created opportunities for Gilbert and her lover to enjoy uninterrupted trysts while medical staff attended to the medical emergencies she created. Lead prosecutor Assistant US Attorney William Welch, said witnesses had reported Gilbert was seen flirting with Mr Perrault and pressing her body against him provocatively during these emergencies.

In court documents it was noted that hospital regulations

required Mr Perrault to perform cardiopulmonary resuscitation during codes, if required by a doctor. Witnesses had told the prosecution team that Gilbert would wipe Perrault's brow as he performed CPR.

It was also alleged that Gilbert would kill her patients so that she could leave work early.

In the case of Kenneth Cutting, 41, on 2 February 1996, Gilbert was keen to keep a date with her lover and actually asked her supervisor if she could leave early if Mr Cutting died. That evening Mr Cutting was the only patient on Ward C, leaving him alone with Gilbert, who was the sole nurse on duty.

It was a strange question but the supervisor reportedly answered, 'Well, yes.'

Mr Cutting went into cardiac arrest soon after and died.

Two days after Mr Cutting's death, Gilbert was working as the medication nurse for 65-year-old Angelo Vella, a former Marine. Prosecutors said Gilbert was supposed to flush his IV site with saline, but when she injected him, he screamed and went into cardiac arrest. Vella was stabilised and allegedly told nurses that Gilbert had injected something into his IV.

On 15 February 1996, Edward Skwira, 69, was brought into the ICU in a stable condition. One hour after Gilbert's shift began, he went into cardiac arrest. Prosecutors alleged that Gilbert was alone with him at the time. He died three days later. Again, epinephrine ampoules were found in the syringe waste bucket following the emergency.

It was also alleged by the prosecution that Gilbert had injected another patient Francis Marier with epinephrine and insulin on 20 December 1995. Marier survived.

Showing the jury a vial of epinephrine, with the photographs of Gilbert's alleged victims on the television monitors scattered around the courtroom, Mr Welch said the nurse had 'transformed this drug from a drug of life into a drug of death, solely for her own personal, selfish purposes'.

As part of the prosecution team's closing arguments, Assistant

US Attorney Ariane Vuono told the court that Gilbert preyed on her patients.

An Associated Press report on 23 February 2001 said that Ms Vuono wagged her finger at the 'bright nurse' and said Gilbert 'knew exactly what epinephrine would do to a person, especially a person in a vulnerable state'.

'These seven victims were veterans,' Ms Vuono said. 'They were vulnerable. They were the perfect victims. When Kristen Gilbert killed them she used the perfect poison.'

Jurors found Gilbert guilty of the murders of Henry Hudon, Kenneth Cutting and Edward Skwira as well as the second-degree murder of Stanley Jagodowski. She was also found guilty of the assault with intent to murder of Thomas Callahan and Angelo Vella but not guilty of the same charge relating to Francis Marier.

Gilbert was reported to have softly wept when the jury verdict was announced on 14 March 2001. She had declined the chance to address the judge.

The widow of Stanley Jagodowski, who was 66 when he died, poignantly told the judge of the effect of her loss.

'I still listen for his key in the door. Now I have to face old age alone,' Claire Jagodowski said.

Assistant US Attorney William Welch, the lead prosecutor, called Gilbert a 'shell of a human being' who was cold and calculating in the murder of her patients.

Gilbert's defence lawyer Paul Weinberg implored the court to not impose the death sentence on his client.

'It is easier to incite good and decent people to kill when their target is not human but a demon,' defence attorney Mr Weinberg said. 'Kristen Gilbert is not a monster, she is a human being.'

On 26 March 2001, Judge Ponsor ordered that Gilbert serve four consecutive life sentences in prison, plus 40 years for the attempted murders of Mr Callahan and Mr Vella.

'I am hopeful ... this will be perhaps the beginning of a better day for so many people who have suffered so much,' Judge Ponsor said.

'It's a very bittersweet day when you think your daughter is going to get life imprisonment instead of the death penalty,' Mr Strickland told the media.

In his 2002 opinion piece in the *Boston Globe*, 'Measuring price of death penalty', Judge Posner commented:

> *Presiding over this, the first death penalty case in Massachusetts in several decades, was the most complicated and stressful thing I've ever done (aside, perhaps, from raising teenagers).*
>
> *Even with considerable circumstantial evidence, including Gilbert's own apparently inculpatory statements, but no eyewitness testimony, the trial presented in large part a classic battle of experts.*
>
> *Never before have I understood so poignantly the devastating impact of a murder. It is hard to lose a loved one, harder to have had no opportunity to prepare for the loss, harder still to know that due to accident or mistake the loss was avoidable. But hardest of all – on a whole other level – is to perceive that the loss came through the deliberate viciousness of another person.*

Kristen Gilbert is held at the Carswell Federal Medical Center in Fort Worth, Texas.

Michael Swango

- Poison Doctor -

When he was a medical student, Michael Swango never really fitted in with his peers.

He was very smart – brilliant, in fact, having graduated summa cum laude (with the *highest* honour) from Quincy College in Illinois before going on to study at the Southern Illinois University School of Medicine. But Swango, born Joseph Michael in 1954 (he was known as Michael or Mike from childhood), was a lazy student. He was working as a paramedic on weekends to make money and he seemed to let his studies slide. The students even coined the word *Swango-ing* for his habit of cramming for exams at the last minute. Swango's skills came up glaringly short compared with the other students at the medical school during the late 1970s and early 1980s.

While Mike was good looking, and could be charming and affable, he was somewhat of a loner. Even more disturbingly, it was noted by other students that he had a fascination with the dying. Although at the time no one thought much of it, many patients whom Swango was assigned to do checks on ended up suffering life-threatening emergencies, and at least five of them died. As a play on the James Bond character, his classmates nicknamed him Double-O Swango as he was acting as if he had 'a licence to kill'.

In general, there was a cloud over Swango's performance during his medical degree and there were some attempts to have him expelled from the course but he managed to hang on (this would become the pattern for his work life). He graduated with his medical degree and started a surgical internship with Ohio State University Medical Center, which was to be followed by a coveted neurosurgery residency.

He only lasted a year and left in mid-1984 at the end of his internship, when the university decided not to continue with his neurosurgery residency. The official reason was that his performance was not up to scratch. The true reason was that whenever Swango was on the hospital floor, otherwise healthy patients started to die.

Swango was placed in the hospital's Rhodes Hall on surgery rotation to start. On 31 January 1984, Swango checked the intravenous (IV) line of Ruth Barrick and asked the attending nurse to leave the room. She returned to find Swango gone and the patient turning blue and suffocating. Doctors were able to resuscitate Ms Barrick but were puzzled as to what had caused her respiratory failure. One week later, Swango answered a call to check Ms Barrick's IV. Once again, after the doctor had left, the patient turned blue. Despite emergency treatment, she died gasping for air.

On 7 February, a nurse saw Swango in the room of an elderly patient Rena Cooper, injecting something into her IV. When he left, Ms Cooper started choking and turning blue. She was resuscitated and recovered. Despite Ms Cooper describing Swango as the person who had injected something into her IV, and the nurse's confirmation, Swango denied being in Cooper's room and the allegations were for the most part ignored.

In the time Swango had been in the hospital there had been an unusual increase in the number of deaths. And most of the patients had all been doing well before dying suddenly and inexplicably. Besides Ruth Barrick, there had been six others, including Cynthia Ann McGee, 19, Richard DeLong, 21, and Rein Walker, 41.

When Swango was transferred to Doan Hall, in another part of the hospital, as part of the surgical rotation, unexplainable deaths began immediately.

On 19 February 1984, Charlotte Warner, 72, was found dead in her room when she'd been doing well following recent surgery. On the same day, Evelyn Pereney started haemorrhaging from places, including her eyes, after being examined by Swango.

On 20 February, Anna Mae Popko, 22, recovering from an intestinal operation, died after being given a shot by Swango.

Officials from Ohio State University conducted an internal inquiry after Swango was accused of putting a toxic substance in the IV of a patient. Despite their suspicions about Swango, he was allowed to continue to practice medicine and the investigation went no further than his dismissal after his internship finished. The university would come to regret not investigating the incidents more thoroughly when its handling of the matter later resulted in scandal and condemnation.

Swango moved back to Quincy, Illinois, the town where he was raised and attended college, and began work as a paramedic in Adams County. In a gesture that appeared to be of goodwill, Swango brought in food to share with his colleagues. After eating some donuts that Swango brought in to work, several of his co-workers fell ill. Brett Unmisig was one of those paramedics and he vomited after eating just one donut. The pair was at a football game the next night and Swango handed Brett a soft drink, after which he fell ill again. The ambulance crew experienced dizziness, nausea, vomiting and headaches – all symptoms of arsenic poisoning. Swango's workmates started to suspect they were being poisoned.

Their suspicions were cemented when two crew members brewed some tea to make a cold iced brew, but had to leave abruptly on a call. They had not sweetened the tea but when they sipped it on their return, it tasted sweet. Swango, who must have heard his co-workers' concerns about the drink, appeared in the room, grabbed the tea and tipped it down the sink.

The paramedics were now frightened and convinced that Swango was trying to hurt them.

They decided to conduct their own investigation and faked an ambulance call that would divert Swango and his partner away from the station for a while. Searching through Swango's bag, they found arsenic-based ant killer that came in the form of a sugar solution (to attract the ants).

Not long after, two paramedics purposely made a brew of unsweetened tea, poured it into two cups clearly marked with the initials of some paramedics and left it in the kitchen where they knew Swango would be alone. They went out on a call and when they returned, saw Swango leaving the car park at speed. The tea tasted sweet again and they raced the sample over to the local hospital for tests, which revealed the presence of a heavy metal. More detailed tests, initiated by the Adams County Coroner's Office, determined the 'sweetener' was indeed arsenic.

Swango was arrested and a search of his apartment uncovered the ant poison; recipe cards to make cyanide, ricin, botulism and pesticide mixtures; guns; survivalist knives; and books on Satanism. A scrapbook was found with newspaper clippings of crime stories, including the 1982 Tylenol Poisonings that to this day, are still unsolved.

The Tylenol Poisonings was one of America's most notorious and frightening crimes. Between 29 September and 1 October 1982, seven people in the Chicago, Illinois area died after taking cyanide-tainted Extra-Strength Tylenol, the top brand of non-prescription pain relief. The poisonings forever changed the way the pharmaceutical and food industry did business. The murders were the catalyst for the introduction of tamper-proof packaging and the incidence of copycat and drug tampering was significantly reduced.

Swango was charged with several counts of aggravated battery and faced trial on 22 April 1985 in front of Circuit Judge Dennis Cashman at the Adams County Court House in Quincy.

The evidence in the scrapbook led some to wonder whether Swango was indeed the notorious Tylenol poisoner.

'Someone, anyone certainly, could contend that that [compiling the scrapbook] was a bit unusual,' Judge Dennis Cashman said while denying the prosecution's effort to introduce the scrapbooks into Swango's aggravated-battery trial.

Swango's co-workers gave testimony during the no-jury two-week trial and revealed a very dark and disturbing picture of Swango. It was noted that he could be extremely professional and possessed a cool and calm head in an extreme crisis. Co-worker Brett Unmisig said in court, 'The worse the call, the better he would act and perform'.

However, Swango often made very inappropriate comments that shocked people around him. For instance, co-workers relayed a comment Swango once made about 'going up to the paediatric ward and killing babies with a .357 magnum'.

Swango dismissed this as simple jesting and testified that 'gallows humour is very common in the paramedic community'.

Another colleague said in court that Swango had once said, 'I feel my life has an evil purpose.'

Other paramedics told of Swango cheering while watching a news report on television of a shooting rampage in California and saying, 'Every time I get a good idea, someone beats me to it.'

As for the presence of the arsenic-based ant killer found in his apartment, Swango said his 'extremely messy and very filthy' abode was the reason. He even claimed he used the arsenic-laced syringes, found during the police search, to squirt the ant poison in the cracks of the apartment walls.

Assistant State Attorney Chet Vahle said the evidence and testimony from witnesses left no doubt that Swango was the one who made his co-workers ill. Mr Vahle said Swango's preoccupation with mayhem was the reason he laced his co-workers' food and beverages with arsenic.

He was found guilty and sentenced to five years' imprisonment. However, Swango maintained he was innocent.

'In no way, shape or form, under no conceivable circumstances,' he said, 'am I now or could I ever be, a danger to any human being on the face of the earth.'

Judge Callahan said he believed that Swango had been using his co-workers as guinea pigs to experiment with the poison's effects. 'I think he wanted to take them to the edge of death. If he had wanted to kill these people, he had plenty enough arsenic to do so,' the judge later commented in a 1999 interview with ABC-TV.

Swango served two years of his maximum five-year sentence and was released from an Illinois prison in 1987.

On his release from prison, Swango set about trying to get back into the medical profession. With a history of poisoning people and also the cloud that hung over him from his university residency days, you'd think it would be impossible.

Not for Swango. A combination of his charm, cunning and lax practices by the medical establishment and colleges, saw him able to work in a hospital setting again.

Judge Cashman, who had sentenced Swango in 1985, received several calls from medical employment agencies about the dubious doctor. Judge Cashman was honest in his character reference of Swango and told Associated Press reporter Sharon Cohen, 'I just told them [the agency] it probably would be wise to stay away from assisting him.' In 1994 Ms Cohen wrote a detailed news story on Swango titled 'Death and Suspicion: The Odyssey of Michael Swango', which was syndicated in newspapers across the United States.

Swango worked for a while as an emergency medical technician in Virginia. He also had a spell at an ambulance company but he was recognised by a hospital nurse who had most likely seen him on television. (In 1986, while still in prison, Swango was interviewed for the highly rated ABC-TV news program *20/20*, where he again denied he had harmed anyone with poison.)

In 1990, Swango legally changed his name to David Jackson Adams so that he could try to weasel his way back into a career as a doctor. He forged several documents, including one from the Illinois Department of Corrections that gave a false impression of his criminal record to read that he had served six months' prison time for a bar-room brawl, rather than the five-year sentence for poisoning.

His name change didn't last long. The fact that his new name was not the same as the one on his medical diploma caused problems and he was forced to reveal his true surname. But Swango was very good at convincing people that he was misunderstood.

Soon after, Swango met Kristin Kinney, a nurse at Riverside Hospital in Newport News, where Swango was doing a refresher course. Swango had been married briefly in 1989 to his girlfriend of six years Rita Damos, who had stuck by him while he was in jail. However, the relationship was volatile and there were accusations of affairs and sexual harassment by Swango towards some of his female colleagues. The couple separated and divorced in 1991. He met Kristin a few months later and the pair became an item. By all accounts from friends and family, Kristin was swept off her feet by the handsome Swango. He took her to concerts, the theatre and showered her with attention – it was a whirlwind romance.

He kept from her the several job dismissals when people found out his criminal past. Kristin was oblivious to her boyfriend's dark past and had fallen in love.

In 1992, Swango was accepted into a one-year medical residency at the University of South Dakota's (USD) Sanford School of Medicine, in Sioux Falls. This was despite the fact the admission faculty staff had discovered Swango had lied about his criminal record *and* had served time.

The director of the program, Dr Anthony Salem, was duped by Swango's story. Speaking to reporter Sharon Cohen for her 1994 Associated Press article, Dr Salem told her, 'You've got to know this guy. He had convinced me not only that he was not guilty … but that it was a total miscarriage of justice.'

'I believed him rather than calling the court and saying, "Send me the documents" … I said, well, shoot. Let's give him a chance,' Dr Salem said.

Dr Salem did do his own checking and discovered Swango had lost his medical licence for an unspecified felony (the poisonings) and had been denied a licence to practice medicine in Virginia (when he'd applied under the changed name David Jackson Adams). However, Dr Salem said he felt Swango had explained the reasons for his troubles.

Following his acceptance in the residency program, Swango proposed to Kristin and she accepted. They moved to Sioux Falls together and Kristin was hired as a nurse at another hospital affiliated with the university.

Swango became known as one of the best emergency-situation doctors the hospital had, and Kristin also thrived in her new position.

However, in October 1992, Swango made an application for membership to the American Medical Association (AMA), even though he was an unlicensed doctor. It can only be assumed he thought they would not check his credentials. It turned out the application actually did require a thorough background check, and the AMA immediately told the University of South Dakota about their new doctor's disturbing past.

The university suspended Swango from the program and the South Dakota Governor George Mickelson requested state officials provide him with a full report on the case and how the doctor came to be employed despite his criminal past.

In 1993, Swango *again* managed to get a job by lying on his application. This time he secured a position in the psychiatric medicine program at the State University of New York's medical centre at Stony Brook, Long Island.

Shortly before he obtained his latest job in New York, Kristin Kinney, Swango's fiancée, was found dead from an apparent suicide. Kristin, 27, always affectionately known as KK to family and friends, had begun to experience depression in the years since she met Swango. In fact, Kristin's family have always suspected that Swango was poisoning her too because before her death, she had experienced debilitating migraine headaches, nausea and disorientation – all signs of arsenic poisoning.

In his book about Swango called *Blind Eye: The Terrifying Story of a Doctor who Got Away with Murder*, Pulitzer Prize–winning writer James B Stewart asserts his belief that Swango was responsible for Kristin Kinney's death. Some of the effects of arsenic – the headaches, tiredness and confusion – caused her to become depressed enough to commit suicide.

On Swango's first rotation of the State University of New York's program, he worked at the Veterans Administration (VA) Hospital in Northport, New York, and again, his patients began to die.

On the first evening of Swango's duty his first patient Dominic Buffalino died mysteriously, even though he had been admitted with only a mild case of pneumonia. Over the next couple of months, a number of other patients died suddenly of heart failure. Included among them were Thomas Sammarco, 73, George Siano, 60, and Aldo Serini, 62. Another patient Barron Harris, 60, lapsed into a coma after being given a shot by Swango, and died soon after.

Meanwhile, Kristin Kinney's mother Sharon Cooper was desperate for answers and wanted to expose the lying medic. She had spent the months after Kristin's death trying to make sense of it and she had concluded that Swango had driven Kristin to suicide. Mrs Cooper knew some detail about Swango's past from what Kristin had told her.

Appalled at Swango's past and the fact he was able to continue to work as a doctor, Mrs Cooper contacted a nurse friend of her daughter who worked at USD's Sanford school. This nurse told the school's dean Robert Talley where Swango was. The university and the AMA had lost track of Swango after he was suspended from the South Dakota residency program.

Dean Talley then contacted his counterpart at the Stony Brook medical school in New York, Jordan Cohen, with the shocking news of Swango's past. Swango was fired from the residency program and just days later, the medical director who had accepted Swango into the psychiatric residency program resigned from his post. Dr Alan Miller acknowledged he had made a mistake not making further inquiries into Swango's murky past.

In October 1994, a federal warrant was issued for Swango's arrest. He was facing charges of falsifying documents in order to enter the service of a federally granted facility – in this case, the Veterans Administration hospital at Stony Brook.

But Swango had vanished. The FBI figured that Swango was either dead or had fled the country.

Swango was on the run. He landed in Zimbabwe in December 1994 and found employment as a doctor at the Lutheran-run Mnene Mission Hospital. To have an American doctor as charming and experienced as Swango was quite the achievement for the small hospital in the isolated town of Bulawayo.

Swango was effusive in his excitement about working in Zimbabwe and helping the 'poor and disadvantaged'. But whether it was Africa or America, Swango's murderous desires followed him wherever he went. In 1995, five patients at the Zimbabwe hospital died under unexpected and mysterious circumstances. Little did they know the new doctor was on the FBI's 'most wanted' fugitives list.

And patients continued to die. The ones who survived told the same story: That 'Dr Mike' was the last person they remembered. One patient Keneas Mzezewa said he awoke one night to Swango putting a needle in his arm. Mr Mzezewa recalled Swango stepping away from his hospital bed and, in a strange and sinister move, was waving goodbye. Mr Mzezewa survived. He screamed at hospital staff that Dr Swango had injected him. Swango denied this to the hospital director Dr Christopher Zshiri, claiming the man must have been hallucinating. However, a nurse had found a syringe cap by the patient's bed.

The incidents were stacking up and far from being a backward health facility that would not have the sophistication to notice Swango's killing spree, the hospital had become highly suspicious of the charming, cool American. Dr Zshiri went to the police with the suspicions about Swango. An official investigation was undertaken and a search of Swango's cottage found lethal drugs and medical equipment.

Swango hired a top lawyer, confident he could make a case of defamation against the hospital but witness statements bolstered the Zimbabwe Republic Constabulary's case against him and inter-country communications meant the truth about Swango's background was now known in other parts of the continent.

Swango failed to appear at a court hearing in 1996 and his trail went cold. He was on the run again, hiding out in Zambia and then in Europe for nearly a year.

The deadly doctor's luck ran out in 1997 at Chicago's O'Hare International Airport. Swango had flown into the Windy City from Zimbabwe and was intercepted as he boarded a flight to Saudi Arabia, bound for a new medical position. He was cuffed in the terminal, read his rights in a private room and told he had been arrested for fraudulently entering Stony Brook and practising medicine without a licence. From Chicago he was transported to New York for trial.

Swango was sentenced on 12 July 1998 for the fraud charge. As part of his confinement at a high-security jail in Colorado, the judge stipulated that the prisoner would at no time be involved with the preparation or delivery of food. Swango's arrest and imprisonment for the fraud charge gave investigators valuable time to keep building their case against him for murder.

Just days away from release from prison in Colorado, Swango was accused of the 1993 murders of three patients at the VA Hospital in Northport, New York. Zimbabwean authorities also charged him with poisoning seven patients, of whom five died.

Announcing Swango's murder indictment, US Attorney Loretta Lynch said he was 'exactly the kind of doctor you would want to avoid. The problem is his appearance, his mannerisms and everything he did was designed to draw people in and make them trust him – when they should not have.'

On 17 July 2000, Swango was formally indicted and pleaded not guilty. However, on 6 September, Swango's legal team made a plea bargain deal that saw him plead guilty to giving lethal injections to the three patients at the VA Hospital. Had he not done so, he faced the possibility of the death sentence in New York and extradition to Zimbabwe.

Swango escaped the death penalty but under the plea agreement he had to travel to Ohio to face questions about the death of a young female gymnast in 1984 at the Ohio State University hospital. He pleaded guilty to killing Cynthia McGee, who was 19 when she died.

Ms McGee was in hospital recovering from an accident when Swango injected her with potassium. The University of Illinois student was on the gymnastics team and had been in the hospital two months since the accident; she had been riding her bicycle and was struck by a vehicle. For prosecutors, it was vital that Swango made the admission about murdering Ms McGee because at that stage, their case relied only on circumstantial evidence, though they were sure the doctor was involved in her death. A nurse had sighted Swango entering her room with a syringe not long before she lapsed into a coma. It is believed that Ms McGee was Swango's first victim.

After Ms McGee died, the driver of the car that struck her bicycle, 17-year-old Scott Bone, was charged with reckless homicide and sentenced to 30 months' probation and 1000 hours of community service, as well as loss of his licence for several years. Mr Bone had a previously clean record and there was no presence of drugs or alcohol in his system at the time of the accident. When Ms McGee died, it was a shock to her family because she had been making a good recovery.

Swango admitted that he had killed the young woman. In 1985, when

Swango was on trial for poisoning his co-workers, Ohio investigators were investigating Cynthia McGee's death and his part in it. At the time, they could not find solid evidence.

A report by Cleveland newspaper the *Plain Dealer* revealed that Swango was asked to draw some blood from Ms McGee for a culture because she was running a fever. However, the medical charts showed blood was never drawn and Swango did not call for help when Ms McGee went into cardiac arrest.

Scott Bone's conviction was upheld on appeal in 1985 and the district attorney in the case said that the young man's culpability would not be reduced if Swango's involvement in Ms McGee's death were proven. However, after Swango admitted to killing Ms McGee and was sentenced to life for aggravated murder (with a 20-year minimum), it was speculated that Bone would try to have his conviction overturned. Bone and his lawyer refused to comment publicly about Swango's conviction for Ms McGee's death.

No one will really *ever* know how many deaths Michael Swango was responsible for. Author James B Stewart suggested in his book that the doctor could have killed as many as 35 people in America and Africa. Stewart's book is the most authoritative account of Swango's crimes, and the medical establishment's 'blind eye' to the murderous doctor's actions.

Rosalinda Conroy, whose stepfather George Siano, was one of the doctor's Long Island victims, told the media, 'Unfortunately there are maniacs like Swango in this world. You just don't think they are going to be your doctor.'

Swango will see out the rest of his life in a maximum security 'supermax' prison in Florence, Colorado.

Sonya Caleffi

- Italy's Angel of Death -

Sonya Caleffi had wanted to be a nurse since she was 12. Although suffering from anorexia and depression, Caleffi did manage to complete her nursing studies. From 1993 to 2004, Caleffi worked in a number of hospitals and nursing homes. During this time she was married and divorced. She continued to be plagued by depression and attempted suicide on a number of occasions. She was also undergoing psychoanalysis.

Caleffi was living in the Como area and working at a new, 900-bed Manzoni Hospital in Lecco, north of Milan, when she was arrested on 15 December 2004 for the deaths of five patients in just one month.

There had been concerns about suspicious deaths at the hospital in the months leading up to her arrest and an internal investigation revealed that Caleffi, 34, was the common link in the five suspicious deaths.

Pietro Caltagirone, the hospital director told the media, 'Death rates on the ward had inexplicably doubled in an isolated series of cases, so we called the police.'

It was alleged that Caleffi killed the victims – three women and two men – by injecting air into their veins. This caused embolism, with the air bubble travelling through the artery and eventually cutting off the blood supply to a particular area of the body.

La Repubblica, one of Italy's daily newspapers reported that Caleffi told police that she 'wanted attention on me because I felt underestimated' (English translation). Caleffi reportedly told police that the victims were elderly patients who would only have lived a few weeks longer.

When police searched her home in Como, they found personal journals that outlined the deaths and her feelings about them. They also found several books with themes of euthanasia, including *Veronika Decides to Die* by Paulo Coelho.

In 2005, Caleffi changed her story and claimed she did not remember anything about her alleged crimes.

At Caleffi's trial, colleagues gave testimony that in each case Caleffi had cleared the hospital room of family members and other staff so that she could be alone with the unsuspecting victim. And every time, Caleffi would then appear shortly afterward 'in an extremely agitated state' and call for help.

On 14 December 2007, Caleffi was convicted of five murders and two attempted murders and sentenced to 20 years' prison. Police had noted that the list of her alleged victims was 'almost certainly much longer'.

Italians were obsessed by the case and Caleffi's name appeared regularly in the media.

In 2008, Caleffi was interviewed exclusively by Italian journalist and television identity Franca Leosini for her popular program *Storie Maledette* (Stories of the Damned). It was the interview many Italian media outlets had been battling to secure. Leosini said it had been 'very difficult' to convince Caleffi to speak on the record.

'The first thing I try to establish is a human relationship with my interviewee. Mine is an approach that requires a deep respect for the person in front of me because, talking to me, they had the courage to descend into the hell of their past,' Ms Leosini explained of her hard-hitting interviews with convicted killers.

On Caleffi, Ms Leosini said: 'And I can say that I found a girl completely different from that which has been described by newspapers and TV.'

From the San Vittore Prison in Milan, Caleffi spoke to Ms Leosini and described her painful adolescence and her difficult relationship with her mother. To escape home, Caleffi married young and the union did not last. She also tried to explain why she had killed people – that she had wanted to feel powerful and important.

'But I did not want to kill,' Caleffi told Ms Leosini. 'I just wanted to make things worse. I created the emergency and then called physicians. I was stuck and I remained watching, I sat on the sidelines …'

'I too am looking [for] answers,' she explained. 'There are no excuses for what I did. It would be wrong not to be strict with myself.'

Caleffi was freed from prison in 2018.

Stephan Letter

- Germany's Killer Nurse -

By his own admission, German nurse Stephan Letter has killed so many people he can't recall the exact number. German society was horrified when Letter was arrested in 2004 and charged with 16 counts of murder, 12 of manslaughter and one mercy killing.

Letter started working at a hospital in Sonthofen, Bavaria in January 2003 and just months later, the deaths started to occur. Sonthofen Clinic had a large intake of elderly patients and the deaths were not initially thought to be suspicious.

Letter killed the patients – many over 75 years old but there were a few who were in their 40s – with an overdose of drugs that he would steal and stockpile at home. When police searched his home after his arrest, they found a quantity of drugs that was capable of killing up to 10 people. In fact, it was the missing medication that proved to be the downfall of Letter. Police were only called to the hospital because drugs had vanished, and had been going missing for months.

Letter told police that he used a cocktail of drugs including the respiratory drug Lysthenon, a muscle relaxant, and tranquilisers for his fatal injections. To investigate this, the exhumation of 42 bodies from the Sonthofen Cemetery was ordered. For the sleepy alpine town, the matter of the killings was very painful, especially as many locals were victims. Letter explained to police that he had wanted to end the suffering of the terminally ill.

Letter's trial started in July 2006. Speaking to the Associated Press at the beginning of the trial, lawyer Wilhelm Seitz, who was representing the families of some of the nurse's victims, said Letter's defence team's claims he was an 'angel of death' could not be believed.

'He acted relatively indiscriminately and aimlessly,' Seitz said. 'Not all of the patients were seriously ill, and he had had no contact at all with some of them.'

Petra Reindl's mother was one of Letter's victims and Ms Reindl told London's *The Times* newspaper that her mother was in hospital for gall bladder pains.

'In other respects she was healthy,' Ms Reindl said.

Letter's final victim, a 73-year-old woman called Pilar Del Rio Peinador, was in hospital for breathing problems but was in much improved health when she was injected by Letter in July 2004. In fact, she was planning a trip back to her native Spain at the time she died and prosecutors used this example to shatter Letter's mercy killing defence.

Another victim was 79-year-old Beata Giehl, who was admitted to hospital with a suspected heart attack on 30 April 2003. Her daughter, Waltraud Schoenberger told the *Sunday Times* that on the afternoon of her admission, Mrs Giehl was upbeat and chatting with her daughters. However, by 10 o'clock that night, the woman was dead.

How did Letter choose his victims? He would loiter in the hospital corridors, eavesdropping on doctors discussing their patients' conditions and their survival chances. Letter would then inject the unsuspecting patient while he was doing his first round of the night shift. On the second round, he would 'find' the patient unresponsive. He would often comfort the relatives of the people he had murdered.

During his trial, Letter's defence brought in psychologists to give testimony about their client's state of mind when he was committing the murders.

Letter, who was described as cheerful, helpful and never reluctant to console grieving relatives, had a dysfunctional relationship with his mother. The defence team told the court that Letter's mother was neurotic and controlling and had diminished her son for years because of her belief that he had a learning disability (Letter had poor coordination as a child). Letter had ambitions of becoming a doctor but these were thwarted by poor school results.

The Times reported that Letter's lawyer Jurgen Fischer said, 'I shall be asking the court to authorise a psychological examination of the young woman to establish how the symbiotic effect of two psychologically damaged people affected the evolution of the crime.'

On 20 November 2006, Letter was sentenced to life imprisonment for his crimes and the judge ruled that no upper limit should be placed on the sentence, which meant Letter could not be released after 15 years, should he have a record of good behaviour. (In Germany, parole is automatically considered at 15 years.)

Letter appeared to choke back tears on hearing his sentence, reported *The Times*'s Berlin correspondent Roger Boyes, and seemed to mouth 'Es tut mir Leid', which translated means 'I am sorry'.

Christine Malèvre

- Madonna of Euthanasia or Angel of Death? -

Frenchwoman Christine Malèvre claimed to have killed out of mercy for her seriously ill patients.

Malèvre worked at François Quesnay hospital, in the Paris suburb of Mantes-la-Jolie, from February 1997 to May 1998. It was the suspicious death on 3 May 1998 of a patient with lung cancer that aroused concerns regarding the 28-year-old nurse. Though the patient Jacques Dutton, 71, had terminal cancer, his medical team had not expected his death for weeks.

There had been simmering suspicions of Malèvre for some time with colleagues troubled that she was regularly administering sedatives. There was also the matter of an unusual number of deaths in her presence.

After the ward's head nurse revealed her concerns to a senior manager, the hospital started to investigate. It was discovered that patients being cared for in the neurology and pulmonology department were three to four times more likely to die while Mademoiselle Malèvre was on duty. She was suspended from her duties in early May 1998, just days after Monsieur Dutton's death. Malèvre attempted suicide at her home by taking a drug overdose.

In July 1998, she was arrested and the case fuelled a nationwide debate in France about euthanasia. The press portrayed Malèvre in a sympathetic light, which garnered support from the public. Malèvre claimed her original confession to 'assisting' in the deaths of up to 30 patients was made under duress. She had admitted to injecting patients with lethal doses of morphine, potassium and other drugs. She was charged with the murder of seven of her patients.

In 1999, Malèvre wrote a book about the incidents called *Mes Aveux* (My Confessions). It seemed a bit strange that Malèvre would write a book so soon after she was charged – and years before she would go to trial – but in past interviews she had explained it was her way of explaining the taboo of euthanasia.

It took almost four years for Malèvre to face trial at the Assize Court (a criminal trial court) of Versailles. In January 2003, her eagerly awaited trial began. While on bail, Malèvre had appeared on television shows and given interviews about her case and the fact that she had wanted to help people end their lives in peace. Malèvre had enjoyed fairly widespread public sympathy and was portrayed as an 'angel of mercy'.

The French Association for the Right to Die in Dignity, which supports legalising euthanasia, believed the Malèvre trial exposed a common practice in hospitals of clandestine euthanasia. The organisation had lent its support to her and used her case as fuel for their cause.

At the time of the trial in 2003, sociologist and pro-euthanasia activist André Monjardet told Radio France that euthanasia was quietly, but regularly, practiced in French hospitals and that a survey found that almost half of French medical practitioners under the age of 55 had either performed euthanasia or expected to do so at some point.

All along, Malèvre had maintained that the patients had asked her to help them end their lives. However, some damning details of the case were leaked to the media, by some relatives of victims, which alleged Malèvre acted without the knowledge of her patients. In other words, the patients had not asked her to help them die; Malèvre had allegedly played God and decided on the fatal course of action.

The pro-euthanasia groups who had championed Malèvre quickly dropped their support and the French media no longer treated her sympathetically.

The Times's Paris correspondent Charles Bremner covered the case.

Benoit Chabert, the lawyer representing the interests of the victims' families, said Malèvre was a serial killer and should be treated accordingly.

'This is the trial of a woman who, while practising her profession of nurse, put people to death,' Monsieur Chabert said.

Olivier Morice, another lawyer for the families, was equally as suspicious of Malèvre's angel of mercy act.

'Christine Malèvre is not the Madonna of euthanasia she makes herself out to be, but on the contrary a woman who is unbalanced and who deliberately overstepped her authority,' Monsieur Morice told French television during the trial.

Malèvre was found guilty and sentenced to 10 years' prison. She was also banned from the nursing profession. Malèvre took her case to the Paris Court of Appeal, which gave her a longer sentence of 12 years. Malèvre reportedly told the court, 'I want to live, live my life as a woman to start a family.'

Pro-euthanasia activists still used the trial to highlight the fact that clandestine mercy killings happened in France.

'It's exactly this type of action we are fighting against,' said Edith Deyris, secretary general of the Paris-based Association for the Right to Die in Dignity, during a television interview after the verdict.

'We want transparency. We want a realisation and concerted action within hospitals – based on written demands of patients who want to die.

'In other words, the complete opposite of the shadows and impreciseness we found ourselves with the trial of Christine Malèvre.'

Malèvre was released in 2007, after four years in prison. French e-magazine *FranceSoir* reported in July 2011 that following her release from prison, Malèvre married and returned to school to study accounting-based subjects.

Timea Faludi

- Hungary's Black Angel -

On 19 February 2001, a 24-year-old nurse named Timea Faludi was arrested and charged with killing eight people by lethal injection while she was working at Budapest's Gyula Nyiro hospital.

Faludi was dubbed the 'Black Angel' by the press, not for her alleged deeds but more her penchant for wearing all-black clothing during her shifts.

In Hungary, nurses must have an order from a doctor before they administer intravenous injections. Faludi was giving out these injections unsupervised during her night-time shifts.

A colleague, who witnessed Faludi giving an injection unsupervised and unauthorised, raised the alarm with management and the investigation started.

The hospital management tried to distance itself from any responsibility for the alleged crimes of Faludi, who had worked there for six years. Hospital managing director Gabor Takacs said a staff shortage meant that nurses often worked unsupervised.

'The people who died were people who would have died anyway,' Mr Takacs said when interviewed by local media in the wake of Faludi's arrest.

Mariann Vadnai, a hospital department manager, told a press conference that there had been no prior concerns about Faludi's conduct.

'She had worked here for six years and was an experienced, professionally well-trained nurse. If you ask us whether she had made any serious mistake that could have alerted us, the answer is no,' Ms Vadnai said.

Faludi told police she believed she had killed 30 or more of her patients between May 2000 and February 2001. (She later recanted that confession and her lawyer claimed his client made it up to sound more interesting.)

The case prompted a national inquiry into the practices in Hungary's state hospitals. The then Hungarian health minister Istvan Mikola said the inquiry was to 'regain the confidence of the public in the health service'.

In December 2002, Faludi was sentenced to nine years' jail. The case was unprecedented in Hungary.

In 2009, Faludi was released early from prison for good behaviour. In a rare interview given to *Bors*, a Hungarian tabloid, Faludi gave some explanation as to why she killed.

'I suppose, everyone has questions, why I've killed so many people. Why I have decided to carry out euthanasia, although I know very well that it is illegal in Hungary,' Faludi said in the 9 November 2009 article.

'My final five killings were done because I couldn't possibly see people in pain and suffering any longer. I suppose, I had too much emotion for the work I was supposed to be doing,' she said.

Faludi said the killings were out of mercy and nothing nefarious. She claims that the overdoses of painkillers she gave were mercy killings.

Faludi recalled one death, that of a woman she referred to as Madame Kati.

'During her last night, when I was working, she was going through the worst period of her life,' Faludi recalled.

'She was in pain and breathing hard so I called the doctor. He prescribed morphine so I gave her a larger dose in the vein. Just before she faded away she became calm and peaceful. It felt right and peaceful, not like I had killed anyone,' she claimed.

Faludi was banned from ever working as a nurse again.

Roger Andermatt

- The 'Deathkeeper of Lucerne' -

The Swiss have a Roger who is beloved, respected and known around the world. Roger Federer, the champion tennis player, is a source of Swiss pride, but there is another Swiss-born Roger who is infamous for being one of the postcard-perfect country's few serial killers.

Between September 1995 and June 2001, Andermatt killed patients in his care with lethal injections, but in some cases by suffocating them with plastic bags over their faces.

Andermatt worked in several nursing homes in the Lucerne region of Switzerland and his victims were all female and aged 65 to 95. The victims were all suffering from dementia or required high levels of care. They were essentially helpless and at the mercy of their caregivers.

Andermatt, then 28, was arrested in June 2001 after the nursing home he worked at became suspicious about a spate of deaths.

Unlike most other countries, euthanasia is tolerated in many Swiss cantons but the act is strictly regulated. (There are 26 cantons or 'states' in Switzerland and each canton has its own government.) Under national law, it is permitted for a doctor to give lethal drugs to a person close to death, and who is in extreme pain. In fact, the person 'assisting' the death need not be a doctor. This is what is referred to as 'assisted suicide'. However, 'active euthanasia' – the deliberate act of a medical professional to hasten a patient's death – is illegal.

Andermatt confessed to killing 27 patients and claimed he acted out of compassion for the dying.

'As far as his motive goes, he is sticking to his previous comments that he acted out of sympathy, compassion, empathy and salvation of the people involved,' said the magistrate, Orvo Nieminen, as reported by the BBC on 11 September 2001.

'On the other hand, he also acknowledged that in several cases he had been overwhelmed by caring for the people involved. He added that in some cases he felt relieved, somehow liberated, after the person had died.'

Andermatt, by this time 36 years old, was sentenced to life in prison in 2005.

Arnfinn Nesset

- Norway's Only Serial Killer -

Before Anders Breivik, who massacred 77 people in a horrific bomb blast and shooting spree in 2011, Norway's most prolific peacetime killer was nurse Arnfinn Nesset. To date, Nesset is Norway's only serial killer.

Arnfinn Nesset was a nurse and manager of a nursing home near Trondheim, Norway when he was brought in for questioning by police in March 1981 over a large order he had made for a drug called curacit (a derivative of curare). It was in fact a journalist who had received a reliable tip from an employee of the home about a nurse who was ordering excess amounts of deadly drugs.

In small doses the drug can be used as a muscle relaxant but will paralyse the respiratory system if administered in larger doses. Curare, extracted from plants, was used as a paralysing poison on the tips of arrows by indigenous South Americans.

Police discovered that the bespectacled and balding 46-year-old had ordered 280 doses of the drug – far more than would ever normally be needed at the nursing home and enough to kill at least 30 people. At first, Nesset said he had bought the drug to kill a pack of wild dogs that was loitering around the nursing home. However, police were then shocked when he confessed to killing almost 30 patients.

Nesset, who was described by psychiatrists as an 'emotional misfit', was charged with the murders of 25 patients from the Orkdal Valley Nursing Home. The victims were aged between 67 and 94 – 11 men and 14 women. Police swiftly began to investigate the deaths of 136 other patients who had come under Nesset's care.

When his identity was revealed to Norwegians via newspaper and television reports, Nesset presented as a lanky, mild-mannered, puritanical man. He was a member of the Salvation Army and had been born out of wedlock in 1936 and raised in an isolated and closed community on the west coast of Norway. An AAP-Reuters article from 13 March 1983 reported that psychiatrists found that Nesset was 'unwanted and emotionally isolated and this created a deep feeling of inferiority combined with strongly suppressed aggressions'.

Nesset later recanted his confession, claiming it was made under duress. Despite his defence's attempts to have him declared mentally unfit for trial, four independent psychiatrists found that he was sane and in full awareness of his actions between 1977 and 1981.

Nesset's trial, which began in October 1982 and concluded in March 1983, was then the longest in Norwegian legal history. A great deal of time was spent arguing over whether the murders could be classified as euthanasia, which would carry a much lesser jail sentence.

Nesset was found guilty of 22 murders and sentenced to Norway's maximum 21 years. (Anders Breivik also received this maximum sentence though it is likely he will never be released as the judiciary has the discretion to extend the sentence.)

Nesset was also found guilty of one attempted murder and of embezzling US$1800 from some of his patients.

Nesset's crimes had far-reaching effects because almost all the inhabitants of the municipality where the nursing home was had family or acquaintances living there.

He was released in 2004 and has slipped into anonymity. It is believed he is living under an assumed name in another Scandinavian country. Nesset still remains much of an enigma, as no one has ever been able to definitively explain his actions. It is thought by police and experts that Nesset killed scores more people over the years that he was a nurse.

Beverley Allitt

- Angel of Death -

In Britain, the term 'angel of death' is synonymous with one name: Beverley Allitt.

Allitt is one of Britain's most notorious prisoners and is being held indefinitely at a high-security psychiatric hospital. In fact, she is probably one of nation's most despised women, along with the late Moors Murderer Myra Hindley, who along with her boyfriend Ian Brady (now also dead), abducted and murdered five children in the 1960s.

Her victims were the most vulnerable – children she was entrusted to care for in her duties as an enrolled nurse. But hiding behind the caring guise of her profession, Allitt did the unthinkable and harmed the youngsters in her care, time and time again. Four children died and several others almost lost their lives and were left permanently physically and intellectually disabled after Allitt injected them with insulin.

As a girl, Allitt was well-liked and didn't give her parents much trouble. She was one of four children of shop worker Richard and school cleaner Lillian and was raised in the village Corby Glen, Lincolnshire. Neighbours recall that the young Allitt was a keen babysitter who loved babies and little children.

Allitt liked attention and often turned up at school with bandages around her arms and legs and told her classmates of the stories of accidents she had endured over the weekend. Not many people who knew her then could look back and say with certainty that there was something 'not right' about young Beverley but some friends wondered what was under the bandages and whether the injuries were real.

The plump and rather unremarkable teen started training to be a nurse in 1988. She had many absences due to 'ill health' and this meant she failed her final exams. Allitt struggled to find a job at the end of the course but the overstretched Grantham and Kesteven Hospital (now known as Grantham and District) finally relented and gave Allitt a position on Children's Ward 4 in February 1991, where there was a severe staff shortage. In fact, Allitt was the only applicant and a particularly poor one at that. It was a sign of the hospital's desperation that she was hired.

Allitt was seemingly well-regarded by her colleagues and the parents of the children she cared for were impressed by the young woman who seemed to be so devoted to her patients and her profession. Allitt was always willing to help and changed shifts whenever asked so that she could help her colleagues out.

Seven-week-old Liam Taylor was the first child to die in unexpected and mysterious circumstances. Liam had been admitted to hospital in February 1991 with a chest infection and his parents were reassured that their baby was in safe hands. After going out for a quick meal, they returned to the hospital to find their son with laboured breathing and turning blue. Liam was stabilised by the staff and he recovered. It was a terrifying experience for his parents.

Baby Liam, now under the one-to-one care of Allitt, who was tasked with watching him closely, suffered another relapse in the middle of the night. Liam stopped breathing for over an hour but was revived and put on life support. His shattered parents made the heartbreaking decision to withdraw their son from the ventilator and he died in their arms on 23 February.

Consultant paediatrician Dr Charith Nanayakkara was concerned and bewildered by Liam's death. He did not feel comfortable with the pathologist's report that stated Liam had died from cardiac arrest and he pushed for a second opinion. Understandably, the young doctor was worried he had missed something, although there was no evidence to suggest this was the case. He asked for a second autopsy to be conducted.

'My requests were completely rejected,' Dr Nanayakkara told the documentary *Crimes that Shook Britain* for the episode on Allitt, which first aired on British television in 2008.

Allitt had started on Ward 4 just two days before Liam's death.

Less than two weeks after Liam's death, 11-year-old Timothy Hardwick suffered what appeared to be a heart attack and died. Timothy had cerebral palsy and was no stranger to hospitals. He'd had a seizure at his home and had been admitted to Ward 4, where he was unfortunately placed into the path of Allitt.

Just three days later, 14-month-old Kayley Desmond had a near-death experience. Kayley had gone to hospital for a chest infection, from which she was expected to recover well and quickly. However, she was cared for by Allitt, who ran frantically to her colleagues for a 'crash team' as little Kayley had gone into cardiac arrest. The team was able to revive her and she was transferred to another hospital.

The staff was bewildered by these emergency events. Two children had tragically died and several more had been near death.

Five-month-old Paul Crampton was admitted into Grantham and District Hospital on 23 March with bronchiolitis, a common respiratory infection in babies and children. Paul was otherwise happy and in good health and spent three days in the children's ward for drug treatment and monitoring.

On 28 March, Dr Nanayakkara, who had just deemed Paul to be fit for discharge within days, came back to find the baby was in an unexpectedly very poor condition.

'I found [Paul] very ill … he was clammy, he was breathing short and fast,' Dr Nanayakkara said in the interview for *Crimes that Shook Britain*.

'He needed immediate intravenous fluid and checking his blood for suspicions of low sugar and any other possible infections… some of the results from the laboratory came back to say that he had significant low sugar. Fortunately I had given the right fluid and he recovered fairly quickly…'

But baby Paul suffered yet another attack. The staff continued to be completely baffled by these attacks. Again, tests showed he had low sugar and he was given emergency treatment and recovered.

Paul's mysterious, rapid health decline and near-death episode made Dr Nanayakkara think about Liam Taylor, who had tragically died just weeks before, and the similarities between the two cases.

At first nobody made the connection, but when Allitt went on three days' leave, all became stable again on the ward. Baby Paul was making a good recovery and there were no more sudden attacks in other children.

Then, unbelievably, Paul had another hypoglycaemic attack and stopped breathing. Allitt had returned to work that same day and had been assigned to give the baby one-to-one care. Paul was transferred to a larger, more specialised hospital. Allitt accompanied Paul and his mother in the ambulance for the journey.

The hospital was on edge and now there were very strong suspicions that the reasons behind the unexplained incidents were sinister and that someone was deliberately setting out to harm the children.

Five-year-old Bradley Gibson, in hospital with pneumonia, suffered a cardiac arrest the day after Paul Crampton almost died. Bradley was revived. Allitt was on duty that night and the poor child suffered another heart attack when she visited his room. He was transferred to another hospital and made a full recovery.

Soon after, two-year-old Henry Chan nearly died. Henry was in hospital after suffering a fractured skull in a fall at his home and had been making a good recovery until he had a sudden attack just like the other children.

Identical twins Becky and Katie Phillips were born nine weeks prematurely in January 1991, and on 5 April 1991, Becky was admitted to Grantham hospital; she had begun vomiting from a suspected milk allergy. One week later, Becky was much better and allowed to go home. Allitt, who had known Mrs Phillips from outside the hospital, had formed an immediate and strong bond with the family. The young nurse became a trusted family friend.

The family had taken Becky home from hospital but she was unsettled and suddenly stopped breathing. Although she was rushed back to the hospital, Becky died. It was heart-wrenching for her parents but more pain was to come. As a precaution, doctors at

Grantham thought it best that the surviving twin Katie be admitted for observation. As the girls were identical twins doctors feared that whatever had been wrong with Becky could also affect Katie.

Unbeknown to anyone, Katie was under the care of the killer who had murdered her sister. Allitt injected baby Katie with potassium and insulin in an attempt to kill her. Parents Sue and Peter had gone to the canteen and when they returned a short time later, Katie was on life support and Allitt told the traumatised couple that she had found the baby not breathing.

Doctors spent almost an hour trying to revive Katie and by the time they got a heartbeat, the tiny girl had experienced so much oxygen loss to the brain that she was permanently disabled from Allitt's attack.

In an interview that ran in *The People* newspaper (now the *Sunday People*) on 31 January 1999, Mrs Phillips recalled that the couple never could have guessed that Allitt had murdered Becky and seriously injured Katie.

'After Becky died Allitt said how sorry she was and not to worry about Katie because she would be fine. She seemed good at her job. You would never think she would harm anybody,' Mrs Phillips told journalist Allison Phillips (no relation).

'I thought when she found Katie not breathing, she had saved her life. We were so grateful we even suggested she could be Katie's godmother,' she recalled.

More unexplained attacks in otherwise healthy patients continued to occur. Michael Davidson, six, was rushed to hospital on 7 April after he was injured in an accident with an air rifle. He was in a serious condition with the pellet lodged in his chest, but was expected to recuperate well. Michael ended up in Allitt's care as he recovered from the surgery.

Michael's father Alan Davidson told *Crimes that Shook Britain* that he was confused as to why his son suddenly had a violent reaction to his intravenous injections and collapsed. Michael recovered but the medical staff was worried by his sudden decline and mystified as to why it had occurred.

Nine-month-old Christopher King, who had been admitted for a stomach problem, suffered a seizure, stopped breathing and turned blue. Eight-week-old Christopher Peasgood was in hospital with breathing problems and was having oxygen treatment when he suffered the same as Christopher King. Then seven-week-old Patrick Elstone, admitted for an ear infection, was 'found' unconscious by Allitt. The oxygen deprivation left baby Patrick with permanent brain damage.

These three boys survived but the next baby to come under Allitt's care would not.

Claire Peck, 15 months, was admitted to Ward 4 for treatment of asthma symptoms. As staff prepared treatment for the little girl, Allitt was left alone with her. Suddenly, she rushed for help saying baby Claire had turned blue and couldn't breathe. She was successfully revived but Allitt was again left alone with Claire while the doctor went to speak with her parents. Claire suffered a second attack and was unable to be revived.

The doctors were now convinced there was a rogue staff member who was purposely hurting the children and the hospital called the police. Lincolnshire Police Detective Superintendent Stuart Clifton discreetly came to meet the hospital and listen to management's concerns.

There was also the fact that days before baby Liam Taylor died, the key to the refrigerator that held medication – including insulin – on Ward 4 had gone missing.

Mr Clifton recalled to *Crimes that Shook Britain* that the last person to have it was Allitt. She had been questioned about this and said she had given it to another staff member (she couldn't remember who) but management had never followed this up.

The results of Paul Crampton's pathology results provided the key to begin to unravel the mystery of the children's collapses. His blood results showed extremely high levels of insulin in some of the samples when there was absolutely no reason why it should have been in his system.

This was the linchpin for police to launch an inquiry into whether the children were being poisoned by someone at the hospital. More blood samples of the affected children showed insulin levels that were unexplainably high.

When officers in the incident investigation team started to plot details like when the health emergencies occurred and what staff members were on duty at the time, it became apparent that one nurse's name stood out: Beverley Allitt.

'The charts showed that on every occasion that there was a child collapsing, Allitt was on duty,' Mr Clifton said.

When Allitt, then 23, was arrested on 21 May 1991, officers were quite shocked at her lack of emotion while being questioned.

Lincolnshire Police officer, Michelle Billingsley, who was working the investigation, said Allitt was unemotional during the interviews and 'gave absolutely nothing away'.

The team had to prove that Allitt was the culprit.

During a search of Allitt's family home, police found a hypodermic needle and an exercise book called an 'allocations book'.

However, it wasn't enough. Police needed more time to build their case and reluctantly, Allitt was released from custody but dismissed from Grantham Hospital. She would not be allowed on Ward 4 again.

Digging deeper into Allitt's background and some of the evidence they found at her home, police discovered the significance of the 'allocations book'. The book was a notebook that the ward sister used to make notes about the children on the ward, the type of care they needed and which nurse was allocated with giving that care. This book became an integral part of the investigation.

There was another chilling incident that showed there was something very, very wrong with Beverley Allitt and that she was dangerous to be around. While on bail, Allitt was staying with the family of her close friend, a woman called Tracy Jobson (the pair were said to have been in a relationship for a time). Miss Jobson's 15-year-old brother Jonathan drank a fruit drink prepared for him by Allitt and complained that it tasted chalky. It was later alleged by the prosecution at Allitt's trial that the he suffered a hypoglycaemic attack and collapsed. (He made a full recovery.)

The investigation continued for months but on 20 November 1991, Allitt was arrested and charged with murdering four children, and attempting to murder and causing grievous bodily harm to nine children.

'For someone to be arrested for murder is quite horrendous but it was absolutely nothing to her, no emotion whatsoever. No fear, no anxiety. Nothing,' Officer Billingsley remembered.

Allitt was remanded in custody for her own protection. Her alleged offences had received national media attention and news footage at the time of her arrest show distraught families and angry people hurling abuse and objects at the police van carrying the accused serial killer.

At Allitt's brief first court appearance on 21 November 1991, the prosecution lawyer Philip Howes told Grantham Magistrates' Court that there would be a risk to Allitt's welfare and safety if she were granted bail.

'Obviously, feeling is running high in the locality, understandably, especially as far as relatives of the children are concerned,' Mr Howes said, as reported by *The Times*. 'There is a clear risk to this woman's safety if she is granted bail.'

It wasn't just children that Allitt had targeted. She was also charged with the attempted murder of two adults. Allitt had worked shifts at an aged care home near Grantham and had been seen injecting 73-year-old patient Dorothy Lowe, who had diabetes. The woman lost consciousness soon after and her blood results showed she had been given an overdose of insulin. Allitt was also charged with the attempted murder of 15-year-old Jonathan Jobson.

Allitt's trial at Nottingham Crown Court was long, complicated and attracted intense media attention. Allitt, who was once very plump, was now in the grips of anorexia and had lost an enormous amount of weight. She pleaded not guilty to all charges.

Allitt was described as 'extraordinarily mentally disturbed' by one of the experts who gave evidence at her trial. She had a history of self-harm that dated back to her childhood.

The trial lasted 13 weeks but Allitt was absent for most of it (nine weeks in total because of her eating disorder) and did not provide any testimony. During that time she was housed in Rampton High Security Hospital. It was deeply distressing for the families and hospital staff that Allitt never gave a reason for her murderous deeds.

Allitt was found guilty of murdering four children – babies Liam Taylor, Becky Phillips and Claire Peck, and Timothy Hardwick, 11. She was also found guilty of the attempted murders of Paul Crampton,

Bradley Gibson, and Becky's twin sister (and Allitt's own godchild) Katie Phillips. Allitt was found not guilty of attempted murder but guilty of causing grievous bodily harm with intent to Kayley Desmond, Henry Chan, Christopher King, Patrick Elstone, Michael Davidson and Christopher Peasgood. On the charges of attempted murder she was found not guilty of attempting to murder or causing grievous bodily harm to Dorothy Lowe and Jonathan Jobson.

Allitt was sentenced to 13 terms of life imprisonment, with a minimum term of 30 years.

Allitt's conviction also led to more focus on the little-known condition called Munchausen syndrome. The condition was identified in 1951 and named after an 18th-century German baron who used to entertain dinner guests with tales of ridiculously exaggerated heroic deeds. Dr Richard Asher (father of Jane Asher, the English model, actress and former girlfriend of Paul McCartney) first published his research in *The Lancet* in 1951 and details of the unusual condition intrigued the medical world. 'The most remarkable feature of the syndrome is the apparent senselessness of it ... Many of their falsehoods seem to have little point. They lie for the sake of lying,' Dr Asher observed.

Munchausen syndrome by proxy (MPB) has been recognised as a form of abuse where a person either fakes or produces illnesses or symptoms in someone else. It is mostly seen in parents harming their children and is now more widely known as 'fabricated or induced illness by carers'.

Expert witnesses suggested that Beverley Allitt would fit the criteria to be diagnosed with both the disorders.

Professor Roy Meadow, an expert for the prosecution and paediatrician who made significant studies into Munchausen syndrome and was knighted for his work, agreed Allitt was 'extraordinarily mentally disturbed' and said that she had a severe personality disorder that could not be cured.

Sir Roy was an often-used trial witness and his 'Meadow's Law' theory – 'one sudden infant death is a tragedy, two is suspicious and three is murder, unless proven otherwise' – was used in several trials of mothers whose babies died suddenly and they were jailed. However, Meadow was later discredited for expert testimony he gave in the case of a lawyer Sally Clark, whose two babies died of unexplained sudden deaths. Ms Clark was found guilty of killing her babies but in 2003 her conviction was quashed because it was decided that a statistic Meadow stated at the trial – that the chance of two children in an affluent family dying of cot death was 'one in 73 million' – was grossly overstated.

The public were shocked and intrigued by the notion that Allitt was suffering from a supposed condition that made a person deliberately harm others for attention.

In a 23 May 1993 article in *The Independent*, journalist Cal McCrystal travelled to Allitt's home village Corby Glen in the week before the killer nurse's sentence to see how the locals were feeling about their notorious neighbour.

Mr McCrystal detailed some of the clues that, in retrospect, could have pointed to Allitt having Munchausen syndrome: 'There were odder things: talking to other nurses, Beverly claimed that a poltergeist had stuck a carving knife into a pillow, set the bathroom curtains on fire and fed tablets to her landlady's dog. At one stage, police were called in to investigate a kitchen fire and the appearance of human faeces in the refrigerator...'

Allitt has spent her sentence, so far, at Rampton Hospital, which is one of three high-security hospitals in England. According to its website, Rampton is split into five areas – mental health, women's services, learning disability, personality disorder and dangerous and severe personality disorder. A 21 August 2002 article in *The Telegraph*, 'Rampton is home to the dangerous and violent', said 'figures supplied by Rampton show that patients stay there for an average of seven-and-a-half years, but a "very small number" are kept there until they die'. Allitt could be one of those 'lifers'.

The killer nurse left a trail of victims – not just the ones she murdered and maimed. Ward 4 was closed down and paediatric services were moved to another hospital. The two paediatricians, including Dr Nanayakkara, who tried in vain to alert management to the possibility that something was very wrong on the ward, were made redundant.

In 1994, the findings of an inquiry into the murders committed by

Allitt, headed by Sir Cecil Clothier, were released. The Clothier Report acknowledged that Allitt's crimes were the product of a deranged and dangerous mind but he also detailed the culture of the hospital and a 'catalogue of lapses' that meant Allitt was able to kill time and again.

The report made mention of the 'general lack in the qualities of leadership, energy and drive in all those most closely associated with the management of Ward 4'.

There were other distressing facts outlined in the report. Allitt's murderous spree could have been stopped after she killed her first victim, Liam Taylor, but the coroner refused requests by Dr Nanayakkara for a specialised post-mortem examination on the baby boy. The report said this decision prevented a line of inquiry that 'could have brought to a halt the whole train of events'.

Imprisonment wasn't the end of the notoriety for Allitt. She remains in the public interest and her victims and their families are permanently reminded of the killer nurse.

The families of the victims have been, and remain, critical of what they perceived as Allitt's cushy life at the secure hospital.

Chris Taylor, father of Allitt's first victim Liam said, 'Where she is now is like being at Butlin's [a famous chain of holiday camps in Britain]. She should be behind bars.'

In 1998, the public were outraged when tabloid newspaper *The Sun* exclusively revealed that Allitt was allegedly enjoying sex romps at Rampton Hospital with her lover Mark Heggie, who was nicknamed 'the Vampire' because he tried to drink the blood from the head wounds of a woman he tried to kill. Heggie, a former slaughterhouse worker, was jailed indefinitely in 1992 for a brutal attack on 63-year-old Alison Da Costa in London.

The Sun article detailed how Allitt and Heggie had ample opportunity for contact, with one visitor telling the newspaper that 'there are discos every Saturday and Sunday, Wednesday bingo and a club at the weekends, plus barbecues, darts, dominoes and pool and pop concerts'.

'They snog, hold hands and she sits on his knee,' the visitor told the newspaper.

In reaction to *The Sun*'s revelations that inmates in Rampton were handed out free condoms and had several perks and activities, Prison

Officers Association spokesman Sean Russell said, 'Sexual activity goes on. Patients have far too many privileges … the problem with management is that they never want to say no. What would happen if somebody like Beverley Allitt got pregnant? There would be a public outcry.'

The newspaper went to the Phillips family for its reaction and father Peter said he thought Allitt should be locked in a cell for 24 hours a day.

'Better still, they ought to let her out and send her back here to Grantham so the parents of her victims can sort her out,' Mr Phillips told *The Sun*.

It was later reported exclusively by *The Sun* in 2007 that Heggie had been moved to another secure unit hundreds of miles away from Rampton.

The Phillips family never stopped fighting for fair compensation for their surviving twin Katie. In 1999, the Lincolnshire Health Authority awarded Katie, then eight, £2.125 million. Allitt had ruined the Phillips' lives and Katie required round-the-clock care for the disabilities she got as a result of the nurse's attempt to kill her.

In 2006, Allitt applied for a review of her sentence. In 2007, the Royal Courts of Justice upheld the ruling that Allitt had to serve a minimum of 30 years in prison for her notorious crimes.

Mr Justice Stanley Burnton said of his decision:

> *I have to say that I regard the determination of the minimum period in a case such as the present – and fortunately cases as extreme as this are rare – as a very difficult task.*
>
> *Once it is accepted that the offender was suffering from mental disorder, difficult ethical and indeed philosophical questions arise as to the degree to which responsibility for the offences in question should be regarded as diminished.*
>
> *I have found that there is an element of sadism in Ms Allitt's conduct and her offending. But that sadism is itself, if not the result, certainly a manifestation of her mental disorder, and it would be unduly simplistic to treat it in the same way as one would if the offender were mentally well.*
>
> *By her actions, what should have been a place of safety for its patients became not just a place of danger, but if not a killing field something close to it.*

Earlier Justice Burnton had said he rejected Allitt's lawyer's opinion that he should take account of the prisoner's progress since the offences. Justice Burnton said the minimum jail period was a reflection of the seriousness of Allitt's crimes and that only 'exceptional progress' could lead to a reduction in the tariff.

'It is not suggested that there has been such progress,' he said.

Some of the victims' families were at the court, including Joanne and Chris Taylor, whose baby Liam was Allitt's first victim.

David Peck, father of Claire Peck, said he was pleased for his family, as well as all the others, that Allitt would spend such a long time locked away.

'We can now put this behind us after 15 years. I couldn't ask for anything better,' Mr Peck said.

Allitt was in the tabloid headlines again in Britain in 2018 when it was reported she was gravely ill with sepsis, also known as septicemia, where the body's immune system attacks tissue and organs as it tries to fight an infection.

A July 2018 online story by Mirror.co.uk attracted almost 100 comments and more than 9800 shares.

With her status as one of Britain's most hated women the comments were predictably brutal.

'Hope the sepsis takes her limbs and then she pulls through,' wrote one reader with the username Muth.

Another user WendyMcA wrote: 'It would be nice if she has to have all her limbs removed and she wakes in agony, and needs everything doing for her, then she can be left in agony and as defenceless as the people she killed.'

More uproar followed when it was revealed on 22 July 2018 a GoFundMe page had been set up asking for donations to help Allitt. GoFundMe is a popular crowdsourcing site where people can raise money for causes.

The page was swiftly pulled down by GoFundMe for violating its terms of service and the incident left many wondering whether the page was started as a joke. However DailyMail.co.uk reported on 24 July 2018 that the account holder had contacted the newspaper to say the account was genuine.

Venerable British journalist Sir Trevor McDonald made a television documentary for ITV, aired on 24 October 2018, called *Trevor McDonald and the Killer Nurse*. He spoke with the surviving victims of Allitt, families of the children she murdered, and police officers who investigated her crimes.

McDonald had covered the Allitt murders when he was a newsreader and remained fascinated with the case.

This deep dive into the investigation reinforced the dedication of the investigating officers who pushed on despite scepticism from some colleagues about the case, with one of the interviewees, Former Detective Superintendent Stuart Clifton telling McDonald that: 'One very senior officer said to me, "you're chasing rainbows". Detectives develop a sixth sense, I think, and particularly experienced detectives, and there was something that just rankled with me that didn't seem quite true.'

The program, part of a series by McDonald called *Crime and Punishment*, included the police interview audio with Allitt that revealed a young woman steadfastly and defiantly sticking to her story that she had not harmed the children in her care.

One of the surviving victims McDonald interviewed was Kayley Desmond. Kayley, who was born with a rare disorder affecting her development, showed McDonald how she still looks under her bed for 'Nurse Allitt'.

Kayley's adoptive mum Sharon Asher said Kayley experienced what could be described as flashbacks about Allitt. Kayley said she was still scared of Allitt 'in case she comes back for me'. Kayley was visibly distressed when talking about Allitt, crying while her parents and McDonald reassured her that Allitt could never hurt her again.

'It's very difficult for her to understand,' Kaley's father Alan told McDonald.

The documentary also explores the controversy over Allitt being detained in a psychiatric hospital, rather than prison – a patient rather than a prisoner.

'She's a murderer; she's a child murderer,' said Bradley Gibson, who was aged 5 when Allitt tried to kill him.

'She's been living the life of Riley in there (Rampton Hospital). She should be serving her life sentences in a prison, behind bars.'

Efren Saldivar

- Killer on the Night Shift -

Jean Coyle was one of a rare bunch. She was the only documented survivor of serial killer Efren Saldivar, a respiratory therapist who confessed to killing more than 100 patients while he worked at a hospital in the Los Angeles suburb Glendale in the 1990s.

Mrs Coyle eventually died in 2003, of the emphysema that meant she was frequently in hospital over the years, usually under the care of Saldivar. In 1997 she actually survived a dose of succinylcholine chloride, a paralysing drug usually used to slow down a patient's breathing when they are about to be put on a ventilator. This type of drug was Saldivar's weapon of choice and Mrs Coyle was one of up to a suspected 50 patients that he killed by lethal injection.

In Mrs Coyle's obituary in the *Los Angeles Times*, her daughter said her mother was a feisty woman who made an impression on hospital staff and this was likely the reason that authorities came to know that she was Saldivar's only known victim who survived.

Saldivar's Mexican parents came to America while Mrs Saldivar was pregnant with Efren and she gave birth in Texas in 1969. To give their new family a better life, the Saldivars trekked to Los Angeles where they worked in unskilled jobs and hoped that their children would get a good education.

Saldivar wasn't a particularly stand-out student at school, although he was intelligent. He did what he needed to get by. Saldivar didn't graduate from high school – not for lack of intelligence but more due to laziness. At the age of 18 he went to a private college in North Hollywood, completed his high school certificate and then studied further to be a respiratory therapist (RT).

Saldivar began his new career in 1989, working close to his home at Glendale Adventist Medical Center (GAMC). As a respiratory therapist, it was Saldivar's job to evaluate, treat and maintain the heart and lung function of a patient. In the United States, respiratory therapists form part of allied health teams in hospitals.

Los Angeles Times journalist Paul Lieberman wrote a series of comprehensive articles on Saldivar, charting his life, the investigation and the trial of the so-called 'Angel of Death'. Lieberman interviewed former colleagues and friends of Saldivar and the picture that was painted showed a man who was amiable, competent and liked to be liked.

In the 28 April 2002 *Los Angeles Times* article 'Graveyard Shift', Lieberman described the culture of respiratory therapists at the GAMC:

> *Respiratory therapists – day or night – were like high school kids. They could be grinds. They could be cutups. They formed cliques and rivalries. Saldivar fell in with the cutups. They might use syringes as water pistols, or drop their pants and moon each other. The RTs worked out of a cluster of rooms on the second floor of the hospital. It was their world apart, with locker rooms for men and women, a lounge and laboratories, offices for their bosses, a 'dirty room' for used implements and a large report room with the assignment board...*

Pranks and dark humour abounded among this group of healthcare professionals. Saldivar was often leading the pack and it became a running joke among his colleagues that he was somewhat of a jinx when he was on shift. It seemed that a lot of Saldivar's patients died during his shift – the graveyard shift.

On one occasion, Saldivar's colleagues accessed his locker to play a prank and actually saw paralysing drugs in Saldivar's locker. They became even more suspicious but did not immediately report the find to hospital authorities because they had accessed Saldivar's locker without permission.

On 3 March 1998, Glendale Police received an anonymous call that Saldivar had 'helped a patient die fast' the month prior.

Police began investigating and on 11 March 1998, Saldivar gave what police later described as a 'jaw-dropping' confession. The detectives were not expecting to hear the soft-faced, cheerful guy confess to a killing spree.

Saldivar waived his right to an attorney and spilled all to the detectives. He revealed that he killed his victims by injecting two paralysing drugs, pancuronium bromide (trademarked as Pavulon) and succinylcholine chloride, into their intravenous lines (IVs). The drugs are muscle relaxants usually used to aid tracheal intubation in patients.

Saldivar said he was a self-styled 'angel of death' who only killed patients who were on the verge of death anyway. In fact, during a polygraph test when asked if he considered himself an 'angel of death', he answered 'yes'.

'We had too much work,' Saldivar stated during the 1998 police interview. 'Only when I was only at my wits' end on the staffing, I'd look on the board. Who do we gotta get rid of? OK, who's in bad shape here?' the *Glendale News-Press* reported in a 2002 article.

Saldivar's registration to practice was suspended days later by the Los Angeles Respiratory Care Board. It was then revoked permanently.

On 27 March 1998, the Glendale Police announced publicly that they were investigating Saldivar's confession.

The media went big on the coverage of Saldivar's self-confessed crimes. He had not yet been charged with any offences and had been in seclusion since the police made the investigation public. The scrutiny of the hospital by the media was intense. How could they have let this happen? The hospital revealed in a statement to the media that it had first heard rumours about hastened patient deaths in April 1997 and that a two-month internal investigation had not found anything suspicious.

Glendale Police officer William Currie was one of the police interviewers and he told the Los Angeles Respiratory Care Board in a statement: 'Saldivar said he felt encouraged by the other therapists at [Glendale Adventist] who would sometimes give him room numbers of patients who needed lethal injections.'

During the extensive police interview Saldivar told Currie that as well as giving patients lethal injections, he also killed patients by suffocating them by decreasing their oxygen supply.

Currie also said that Saldivar 'prided himself in having a very ethical criteria as to how he picked his victims'. Saldivar revealed that he had strict criteria on who he would kill: they had to be unconscious, they had to have a 'do not resuscitate' order in place and they had to look like they were ready to die.

Amid the allegations, the hospital board suspended the whole respiratory care department – a total of 44 people, including Saldivar.

One of Saldivar's colleagues Ursula Anderson, who had worked alongside him on the graveyard shift, was fired by the hospital (along with three other RTs), told the *Los Angeles Times* in 1998 that she was a scapegoat in any alleged wrongdoing that had gone on within their department. Ms Anderson said when she was questioned by lawyers and hospital investigators, they concentrated on images drawn on the respiratory therapists' whiteboard, which depicted, as described by the *Los Angeles Times*, 'frowning faces – drawn with Xs as eyes and a tongue sticking out of a down-turned mouth – next to patient names'.

'The attorney asked me if this was a sign for Saldivar to go and see the patient,' Ms Anderson told the newspaper. But she told them she thought it was merely 'a dark-humoured indication that a patient had died'.

However, it was later revealed that Ms Anderson was romantically involved for a time with Saldivar and she actually told investigators that she had provided him with some of the drugs that he used to kill. Ms Anderson also said she knew that her colleague and lover was injecting patients with the paralysing drugs and had some suspicions that he was killing patients.

She told Glendale Police that Saldivar had killed patients to relieve his workload. The *Glendale News-Press* reported when an investigator asked, 'Did he actually tell you ... he was killing patients because there simply were too many patients for too few therapists?' Anderson replied, 'Yes.' This information was taken from police records that were released by a judge in early 2001.

Saldivar appeared on the top-rating ABC-TV news program *20/20* on 9 April, and publicly retracted his statement that he had made to police about killing up to 50 patients. He told interviewer Elizabeth Vargas that he had made everything up because he wanted to be sentenced to death as he lacked the courage to end his own life. He told Ms Vargas that he needed to make the story as big as possible to warrant the death penalty and that even he had been surprised at how his story had evolved.

On the program *Extra*, Saldivar reiterated that he was depressed and suicidal. 'I lied. I fabricated the confession.' Saldivar said. 'I want to set things straight, I still have a conscience.'

The police were aware that he was to appear on television but were not concerned. It appeared that Saldivar was creating greater suspicion, and more media intrigue about his alleged activities by changing his story.

The case was unprecedented for the Glendale Police Department (PD), which was tiny compared to the much bigger Los Angeles Police Department. Glendale PD had handled eight new homicides in 1997 and now they were looking at a potential 50. The police referred to it as a 'whodunit reversed' where they had the suspect but were now backtracking and searching for the victims of Saldivar's alleged crimes.

To find stronger evidence of Saldivar's alleged crimes, police decided to exhume the bodies of patients they believed could have been murdered. In the weeks after Saldivar confessed to police about his killing spree, a team of four retired doctors spent time with families who feared their loved ones had been killed by the rogue respiratory therapist. There were 350 families that called in and the team of doctors met with them to review medical charts. After about 100,000 pages of patient records were examined, it was determined that the bodies of 20 patients who had been treated by Saldivar and had died suspiciously would be exhumed.

The first exhumation took place one year after Saldivar first confessed to the murders. Forensic experts tested for traces of the muscle relaxant drugs succinylcholine chloride and pancuronium bromide, though it was not known whether traces of the drugs would be detectable in victims who had been buried for two years or more. Certainly, succinylcholine chloride was known to break down and its presence almost impossible to prove. The test for this particular drug was also deemed too unreliable.

Task force supervisor Sergeant John McKillop told a press conference just days before the first exhumation on 30 April 1999, 'If we find [these] chemicals in the tissues…the only logical conclusion would be they were given illegally.'

The *Los Angeles Times* reported that the court-ordered exhumations were scheduled to be done at a rate of one or two per week for several months and that the police said it could take up to nine months to test all samples.

Dr Brian Andresen, of Lawrence Livermore National Laboratory's Forensic Science Center (LLNL), was the forensic chemist who was tasked with testing the remains of the patients for the presence of pancuronium bromide. The LLNL is based in Livermore, California and was set up in 1952 at the height of the Cold War to meet the United States' urgent national security needs of the era. Today, the laboratory's mission is to improve the United States' security through scientific research and engineering development.

Dr Andresen had spent gruelling 16-hour days trying to find a way to extract the drug from tissue samples of the deceased. Eventually he successfully extracted pancuronium bromide from pig livers using polystyrene divinylbenzene, which was originally used to detect the presence of chemical weapons in human bodies.

In terms of its experts in toxicology, Sweden was ahead of many other countries. In the case of Texan killer nurse Genene Jones, a tissue sample of her 15-month-old victim was sent to Sweden in 1983 to be examined by Dr Bo Holmstedt (1919–2002), who was the only doctor in the world at the time able to test for the presence of the muscle relaxant drug succinylcholine chloride in embalmed tissue.

Investigators remained tight-lipped about the case. It took a number of years to build the case against Saldivar and primarily it was the work of Dr Andresen that cemented the case against him.

Dr Andresen found six positive results for pancuronium bromide out of 20 autopsies and his stunning finding was reviewed by another leading toxicologist Dr Graham Jones, who agreed with him that these patients had been murdered. The victims had all died between 30 December 1996 and 28 August 1997.

In a press release issued by the LLNL on 1 April 2001, Dr Andresen's pivotal work in the Saldivar case was explained:

Special analyses by the centre gave Glendale investigators evidence they could use to arrest Saldivar and charge him with the murders of six patients...At the request of Michael Peat, then president of the American Academy of Forensic Sciences, Andresen travelled to southern California to assist in the autopsies of the exhumed remains of some of the 'most mysterious' of the Glendale deaths...Because succinylcholine chloride breaks down quickly into chemicals normally found in human tissue, Andresen concentrated on Pavulon, a potent, synthetic muscle relaxant often administered in low doses to patients on artificial respirators. He found 6 positive results for Pavulon out of 20 autopsies.

In early January, Saldivar was rearrested, based primarily on Andresen's findings...

In his own words in 2004 for the US National Library of Medicine's 'Visible Proofs' exhibition (about the history of forensic medicine), Dr Andresen recalled the moment he found the presence of Pavulon: 'I got a hit...and it took the wind out of my lungs. It was a real homicide...the patients had died a terrible death.'

In a later interview with journalist Robin Mejia for a September 2004 article in *Popular Science,* Dr Andresen said to die of pancuronium bromide poisoning would be 'the most frightening death'.

'If you get injected with it, it makes it so the muscles can't move. Your lungs would stop working, but you wouldn't be able to signal for help. Your death, when it was discovered, would look natural,' Dr Andresen explained.

Now Dr Andresen's method of testing for pancuronium bromide murders is used worldwide.

From his experience, Dr Andresen told Ms Mejia that he thought hospitals should be more careful about storing drugs like Pavulon and that drug companies should add tracers to their products.

In the meantime, Saldivar did a series of jobs – as a detailer at Budget Rent-a-Car, pizza delivery guy, and telephone customer service representative. Saldivar dated a woman who wanted a future with him but he didn't want to bring children into the world with so much uncertainty. Saldivar had failed to mention the 'angel of death' matter that was lingering in his background, threatening to surface at any moment. He had to fess up to his employers at the telephone company after it became known that several families whose loved ones had died in hospital had filed wrongful death suits against him. He left the job.

When Saldivar was finally rearrested and charged in January 2001 with the murders of six people, he was working as an apprentice electrician and had no fixed address. By then Saldivar was 31. It had been the news the families of the victims had been waiting for.

It was up to Superior Court Judge Lance Ito to decide whether to unseal indictment transcripts from a previous grand jury, which would then become available to the lawyers and media. There were more than 100,000 pages of transcripts for the case. (Judge Ito came to be an internationally recognised figure after he was the judge in the notorious OJ Simpson murder trial in 1995.)

The testimony from his fellow respiratory therapists was not only damning for the accused killer, but also for the profession. The revelations came from grand jury transcripts that were unsealed for the trial.

Respiratory therapist Al Acosta's testimony explained that when a patient died, Saldivar would erase his or her name from the therapists' white board. *Glendale News-Press* reported that one time Acosta asked Saldivar what had happened to a patient, and Saldivar mimed 'pushing a syringe' with his fingers.

In his March 1998 police interview, Saldivar had said that apart from injecting around 50 patients, he had also caused the deaths of additional patients at several other hospitals he moonlighted at, which were located in surrounding areas. Saldivar said that by not properly doing his duties as a respiratory therapist, such as performing CPR, he thought he had helped 200 people to die.

'By law, we have to go through the procedures – go through the steps. I'll do…not the greatest CPR, not the best compressions. Or maybe just angle it a little,' Saldivar allegedly told police, as reported by *Glendale News-Press*.

Saldivar pleaded guilty to six murders in a move that spared him the death penalty – and also avoided a very long and difficult trial. It was after this plea that more information came to public light – there was no doubt that Saldivar was a cold-blooded killer.

His initial confession in 1998 was blown out of the water with a second one he gave police after his rearrest in 2001. In his second confession, Saldivar gave a far more clinical retelling of why he killed.

Glendale Police Captain Jerry Stolze said Saldivar told police he stopped keeping track after he killed his sixtieth victim, which was around 1994.

It appeared from his confession that some victims died because the hospital was busy. Others died because they were so ill they were likely to create extra work for him.

On 19 March 2002, *Glendale News-Press* reported that Captain Stolze said that Saldivar was 'very vague' and had difficulty remembering specific names or dates.

'He didn't want to get that personal with the issue,' Stolze said. 'He didn't want to know or remember the names of his victims.'

Shockingly, Stolze also said that Saldivar likened killing to shoplifting chewing gum in that after the initial shock, it was something that he simply got used to doing and commented that once it was done 'you don't think about it for the rest of the day, or ever'.

On 17 April 2002, Judge Ito sentenced Saldivar, who was by now 32, to six terms of life without parole for the murders of six patients: Eleanora Schlegel, 77, Salbi Asatryan, 75, Jose Alfaro, 82, Luina Schidlowski, 87, Balbino Castro, 87, and Myrtle Brower, 84. He was also convicted to one term of 15 years for trying to kill a seventh patient – Jean Coyle.

Judge Ito took time to praise the 'tenacity' of the prosecutors for bringing the case to a close. Judge Ito also said the plea bargain deal that was nutted out between the legal teams had prevented a very long and difficult trial. He noted that many had believed the case was 'a lost cause years ago' and that Saldivar came close to never facing justice.

'This, above all, was a very human tragedy,' Judge Ito said. 'I think nothing more needs to be said.'

The *Los Angeles Times* reported the day after the sentencing:

> *Had the case gone to trial, public defender Bradford was expected to challenge the legitimacy of Saldivar's confessions, both given without a lawyer present. In addition, while Saldivar spoke in general terms about killing scores of patients, he offered no patient names or dates, even after he was shown the medical charts and photos of the people he was suspected of murdering...*

After his sentencing, the serial killer apologised to his victims.

'I know there is nothing I can say to them that can soothe their anger or bring relief to their anxiety,' Saldivar said.

'I want to say that I am sorry. I am truly sorry and I ask for forgiveness although I don't expect any.

'I know I will live the rest of my days atoning for the actions I have committed,' the killer said in a soft voice, as reported by the Associated Press.

Jean Coyle was not happy with Saldivar's sentence. As his only known surviving victim, Mrs Coyle was in the unique position to truly know the horror of the killer's actions.

'I don't know if he thinks he's God or what but it wasn't right,' Mrs Coyle told a media pack after the sentencing.

'I think he should get more than the sentence. I think he should die.'

Saldivar's former graveyard shift colleague Ms Anderson continued to work as a respiratory therapist but in June 2002 the state Respiratory Care Board finally started moves to suspend her license because she failed to report her suspicions about Saldivar.

It had taken several years for any action to be taken, much to the frustration of the Glendale Adventist facility; however, the delay was due to reluctance by state officials to do anything that would interfere with Saldivar's criminal case. Once he had been sentenced, the board made their move to discipline Anderson and the other three RTs who has been fired from GAMC in the wake of Saldivar's original 1998 confession.

Anderson was given immunity from criminal prosecution in exchange for her information on giving Saldivar the drugs that he used to kill patients.

She is used as an example in a book *The Respiratory Therapist's Legal Answer Book* (published in 2006) on why it is necessary for any RT to obtain legal counsel if being interviewed by police or by professional board regulators or investigators. The book reprints some of Anderson's grand jury testimony and states: 'It is never-repeat-never in your best interest to talk to a board investigator without counsel, even if you are not the person being investigated. Do not waive that right. If you say something inappropriate, you might wind up being a target of the investigation too…'

Her grand jury testimony clearly states that Anderson knew Saldivar was killing patients with a paralysing drug and also that she was in a sexual relationship with him at the time she handed him a vial of succinylcholine chloride.

Saldivar's actions left other respiratory therapists disgusted and alarmed. In one letter to the editor, published in the *Los Angeles Times* on 4 May 2002, Michael Ryan of Venice, California (a registered respiratory therapist with 14 years of experience) wrote: 'Not only does Saldivar represent a human failure but also the failure of a respiratory department to exercise cross-checks within the department itself. He has single-handedly given a black eye to an honourable profession that, in my experience, has always exercised the highest degree of professional and personal integrity.'

In 2003, Saldivar said he would pay the families of four of his victims US$20 million to settle their wrongful death lawsuits against him. The hospital was not involved in the lawsuits because too much time had elapsed since the patients died for the families to make their legal claims. It is unclear how Saldivar will ever pay the money to the families. However, the families' attorney thought future payments for his story could contribute to the settlement.

Saldivar is serving his sentence at Salinas Valley State Prison in Soledad, California and will die in jail.

Vickie Dawn Jackson

- The Unassuming Killer -

The hospital in the tiny Texas town Nocona saw more than its expected share of death in a two-month period in December 2000 and February 2001.

When hospital administrators twigged that the death rate for that eight weeks was twice as high as usual they set out to investigate the cause. Predictably many of the unexpected deaths at the 38-bed hospital were traced to the same shift, which helped them to pinpoint the unthinkable – that a nurse was killing patients.

Vickie Dawn Jackson had lived in Nocona, which has a population of just over 3000, since she was a teenager, when her parents moved the family from Indiana. The town is best known for Nocona Boots, a company now owned by the Berkshire Hathaway Group, which makes cowboy boots and has done since 1925.

Jackson was considered to be a pleasant girl. Not a cheerleader, or one of the popular crowd, Jackson blended into her surroundings. She married while she was still in high school but it didn't last and the pair divorced.

She met her second husband Leroy Carson when she was just 19 and they quickly had a child together, a son Curtis in 1985, followed by a baby girl Jennifer in 1986.

Jackson's life was no different from millions of others – a hardworking mum juggling parenthood, taking care of a home and trying to nurture a relationship that wasn't really very good. And she did this all while attending part-time nursing school to become a licensed vocational nurse (LVN).

Jackson had been employed at the Nocona hospital since 1984. She had first worked at the town's nursing home and had worked her way up to nurse's aide, before completing her studies to become an LVN. It was a tough and thankless gig, but Jackson always seemed to be a caring, devoted worker and her patients and their families – all of them from the small town – spoke highly of her dedication.

Jackson and Leroy divorced in 1996 and she married her third husband, Kirk Jackson, soon after. Kirk worked as a nurse's aide at the hospital.

According to Jackson's daughter, Jennifer Carson, in a 6 February 2005 Associated Press report published in the *Lubbock Avalanche-Journal*, her mother's new husband was abusive and the two children moved back with their father Leroy.

The article said:

> By all accounts, 2000 was a hard year for Jackson: she lost custody of her children, a close relative died and she suffered a miscarriage after fighting with her husband, Jennifer Carson said. One day, Jackson told her daughter she'd talked to a psychiatrist who diagnosed her with bipolar disorder.
>
> 'I said, "What's that?" She said, "I could kill you and get away with it",' Jennifer Carson said.

The killings (that are known) of started on 11 December 2000 when Jackson injected a syringe filled with mivacurium chloride (a drug used to suppress breathing when a patient is being intubated) into the intravenous (IV) line of a 100-year-old woman Donnie Jennings.

Jackson's killing spree had begun.

In his extensive 2007 feature on Jackson entitled 'Angel of Death', legendary Texas journalist and writer Skip Hollandsworth detailed the indiscriminate and callous way she killed her victims. Hollandsworth interviewed Jackson in prison for the feature, which was published in *Texas Monthly*. Details of Jackson's victims – names, ages and medical conditions – were detailed in Hollandsworth's exhaustive article.

A week after murdering Mrs Jennings, Jackson killed two people in one shift – 87-year-old Elgie Hutson, who was in hospital with a broken leg, and 62-year-old Sanford Mitchell, who was suffering from cirrhosis.

On Christmas Eve (in a move that was anything but festive), Jackson fatally injected 50-year-old Barbara Atteberry, who was in hospital due to back pain. Jackson then went on to kill 87-year-old Boyd Burnett.

Jackson was stealing drugs and dangerously roaming the hospital for victims, but her style was subtle. After she had given patients the injections she would wander over to the nurse's desk or find a doctor and tell them to check on a patient or that she thought someone had died. There was no rushing about or creating dramatic scenes.

On 29 December, 80-year-old James Gore and 79-year-old Gertie Matthews were murdered by Jackson. They were elderly but not suffering from life-threatening illnesses where a mercy killing could be given as an explanation for Jackson's actions.

One victim, Jimmy Ray Holder, was injected and died while his wife was sitting at his bedside.

Jackson's next victim was 95-year-old Oma Wyler, who had suffered from congestive heart failure. The mother-of-six was strong though, and had recovered, and had been preparing to go home when she unexpectedly died.

The 11 January 2001 saw two men killed within hours of each other – JT Nichols, 82 and John Williams, 78.

With Jackson trawling the hospital, syringe in hand, it appeared that her choice of victims was indiscriminate but in actual fact she often targeted people she knew. People who had slighted her, ignored her or been rude found themselves dead or coming close to losing their lives. In the case of John Williams, it was later revealed that Jackson had gone to school with his son Pat. She had thought Pat Williams was cute, but he hadn't taken any notice of her.

Victim Orvel Moore, 82, had, according to Hollandsworth's article, called Jackson a 'fat ass'. He was injected and died.

Jackson injected Lydia Weatherread, 14, as her mother sat by her bedside. Lydia was in hospital with appendicitis. Her mother screamed that her daughter could not breathe. Doctors rushed into the room and were able to revive the girl. 'Lydia knew Vickie's children: According to school gossip, she had recently turned down Curtis [Jackson's son] for a date ...' Hollandsworth wrote in the *Texas Monthly* feature.

Donna Curnutte, 46, was Jackson's next victim. She went into a coma and died a few weeks later. Moments after Jackson injected Ms Curnutte, she administered another injection into the IV of Lisa Pelkey, 35, who knew Jackson from a bar the women both frequented.

Then Jackson killed closer to home. Lifelong farmer EE 'Preacher' Jackson, 91, was her estranged husband Kirk's beloved grandfather. Kirk Jackson was devastated by his grandfather's death on 4 February 2001. Jackson had calmly killed the old man with a fatal overdose.

The suspicions of hospital administrators were raised when it was noticed that a vial of mivacurium chloride was missing; it had been taken from a crash cart sometime during the overnight shift on 30–31 January. It was noted by the administrators that not only had Jackson been working at the time of every respiratory arrest that had recently occurred, but she was also often the last staff member to check on the patients who had died.

Unaware that she was being watched closely, Jackson tried to kill once more. Donnelly Reid, 61, was resuscitated by staff on 17 February, after Jackson told them to check on the man because he was making a strange noise.

Mr Reid told Hollandsworth for his feature article that when the doctors and nurses who had resuscitated him asked him what had happened, he said a blonde nurse had come in and put something into his IV. She smiled at him and asked, 'Can I do anything else for you?' Shortly afterwards Reid had difficulty breathing. 'I felt like a spring was uncoiling in my head. I couldn't breathe,' he recounted to Hollandsworth.

Officials said upon further investigation in the hospital, they discovered that at least 10 vials of mivacurium chloride were missing from crash carts.

A discarded syringe that contained traces of mivacurium chloride was found at Jackson's home in February 2001. Neither she nor Kirk could tell the police why the syringe was at their home. They were both fired from the hospital.

As is the case with investigations into medical murders, this took some time to investigate. There are almost always exhumations and in this case, 10 patients who died at Nocona hospital in the three-month period in question were exhumed and their bodies tested for the presence of mivacurium chloride. Their causes of their deaths were changed to homicide after autopsies revealed that all died of toxic effects of the drug.

On 16 July 2002, Jackson was arrested and charged with 10 counts of murder.

Her nursing license had been suspended in August 2001 and in the time between then and being charged with multiple murders, Jackson worked in various jobs, most recently a deli in the town of Bowie, near Nocona.

Deli manager Peggy Guzman expressed her shock about having an serial killer on her payroll. Ms Guzman told Associated Press that Jackson denied having anything to do with the deaths.

'She was delightful and loved telling funny stories,' Guzman told Associated Press. 'You just have to know her. They have the wrong person.'

At a press conference the next day to announce Jackson's arrest, Montague County District Attorney Tim Cole praised the cooperation of the staff and administration of Nocona General Hospital.

'Indeed, they made it possible for us to move quickly and for the investigators to move quickly in this case,' Mr Cole said.

'One of the reasons why, in fact, the primary reason why this case was solved was because they let law enforcement know quickly that something was going on at the hospital, and made it possible for us to collect the evidence that we feel will lead us into trial.'

The hospital's former administrator Charles Norris (whose departure was not related to the deaths at the hospital), said all the deaths were on the night shift that Jackson worked, from 7pm to 7am.

'There was one shift where she wasn't scheduled to work that night and they called her in and, lo and behold, they had a couple of codes [medical emergencies],' said Norris. 'It's one thing that pointed us in that direction.'

Michael R Graham, the hospital's CEO, told Associated Press in July 2002, 'When you have an alleged serial killer working in your hospital, it doesn't matter what policies and procedures you have in place. That person's going to do what they're going to do.'

It wasn't clear why Jackson had gone on her calculated killing spree – she wasn't talking. However, some experts believed they had some clues.

As reported by Associated Press in a 15 October 2006 article, FBI special agent David Burns had given testimony at the 2002 grand jury that the 'patients, who had minor ailments and were about to be released, were "high maintenance" and angered Jackson'.

In 2004, Dr Lisa Clayton examined Jackson for a court-ordered psychiatric evaluation and found that the nurse enjoyed having power over others and had a grandiose sense of self-importance.

Jackson was denied bail and imprisoned until her trial in 2005. The trial location had to be moved from Montague County, where Nocona is located, to nearby Archer County because so many potential jurors were likely to have known Jackson and some of her victims. The media were covering the case and there had been a lot of publicity locally, as well as national news outlets.

In a blow for Jackson, her daughter Jennifer, 18, told Associated Press in the weeks before her mother's trial, 'I don't know if she did it or not, but she's perfectly capable of it.'

Jennifer also said her mother 'had a baby face on the outside but was hell on the inside'.

Jackson's trial got off to a shaky start with a mistrial declared on 14 March – the first day of proceedings. In his opening statement, county prosecutor Ralph Guerrero said, 'One question that is going to remain unanswered and the defendant may never answer…' Associated Press reporter Angela K Brown, who was at the court, wrote, 'Defense attorney Bruce Martin interrupted Guerrero, objecting that the prosecutor's remark improperly indicated Jackson would testify. The defendant in a criminal case is not obliged to testify...'

A new trial was scheduled but just as jury selection was underway, again, in October 2006, Jackson made a surprise decision.

It was the knowledge that her daughter could be called to testify at the trial that prompted Jackson, then 40 years old, to plead no contest to the charges of murder on 3 October 2006. It was not an admission of guilt by Jackson but it would ensure she spent probably the rest of her life in prison.

Her attorney Roger Martin said, 'By not admitting guilt and by keeping her daughter out of the mix, she's making herself happy with what happened. She felt this was the best route to take.'

Instead of a lengthy jury trial the judge would make the decision on Jackson's guilt after hearing the prosecution's case. It would be a one-day hearing that would end with an automatic life sentence for Jackson.

'For five and a half years I've never talked to anyone, and I wanted people to know it wasn't me,' Vickie Dawn Jackson told the Associated Press as she awaited transfer to a state prison. 'I feel sorry for the families, but I can't show remorse for something I didn't do.'

Jackson will spend the rest of her life in prison and is currently housed at the Christina Melton Crain Unit in Gatesville, Texas.

Robert Diaz

- The Lidocaine Killer -

Nurse Robert Rubane Diaz claimed it was a 'jinx' that so many patients happened to die on the overnight shift that he worked. He said the hospitals must have had 'bad drugs'.

Diaz came into the profession as a mature-age student. He had started medical studies in the hopes of becoming a doctor, but did not complete the course. He was 40 years old when he finished his nursing studies and started work in hospitals in Riverside County, California. He began working the night shift in the intensive care unit (ICU) of the Community Hospital of the Valleys. The hospital was in Perris, a rural desert city built around the California Southern Railroad when the company built tracks through the area in 1882.

Diaz (also known as David Robert Diaz) only worked for three and a half weeks at the 36-bed hospital during March and April 1981 but during that time, 13 patients in the ICU suffered severe seizures, followed by respiratory and cardiac arrest, during the night shift. Nine of these patients died. The death rate was unprecedented for the small community hospital that had only had six patients die in the whole of 1980.

The hospital closed its ICU in the wake of the puzzling deaths and Diaz moved on to work at San Gorgonio Pass Memorial Hospital, another small, rural facility, in the town of Banning.

Within days of Diaz arriving, patients started to die in the same manner as the unfortunate souls at the Perris hospital. Investigators began to look at 24 suspicious deaths at the two hospitals.

On 13 May 1981, California health department officials forcibly closed the Community Hospital of the Valleys. A United Press International report stated that officials believed the hospital posed a serious threat to public safety.

The small town of Perris was now the subject of statewide – and even national – media coverage. Locals were upset that their town was the subject of a gruesome investigation into the strange deaths of the elderly patients at its tiny hospital.

The *New York Times* visited the town and spoke to some residents. Penny Brechtel, the executive secretary of the Perris Valley Chamber of Commerce, told the newspaper for a May 1981 article, 'It's a mystery all right, but other than going slower past the cemetery when they were doing the exhumations, I haven't noticed things are too much different … well, one thing's for sure: Perris is on the map.'

Another resident Jim Adams, who worked in insurance and was on the city council, said the notoriety was no good for the town. 'It makes us look like a bunch of ninnies with nobody paying attention to what was going on at the hospital,' he told the media.

At the beginning of the investigation Diaz wasn't the only hospital staff member on the radar, though he certainly was the main focus of attention, as he was the only link between the two hospitals' intensive care units.

In retaliation, Diaz filed a US$100 million civil rights suit against Riverside County claiming his career had been ruined by the hospitals linking him to the deaths. At the time he filed the suit, Diaz had neither been named an official suspect nor charged with any crimes. However, his name had been freely mentioned in newspaper articles about the long-running hospital saga. (This lawsuit was later dismissed.)

'I didn't think a thing like this happened in this country,' Diaz said. 'I felt like I got hit by the Gestapo troops.'

Diaz maintained that the deaths were caused by 'bad drugs' at the hospital.

'Every morning when I got off I would say, "What the hell is going on at that place?"' Diaz told a press conference.

Investigators were also looking at the records of several other hospitals and at some other employees, in particular one doctor who was in charge of the ICU in Perris and had signed the death certificates of most of the people whose deaths were being investigated. This doctor, Noberto Babiera, had refused to cooperate with investigators. Authorities stated that this doctor was not the subject of an investigation, yet it frustrated them that he would not help.

In a 20 May 1981 Associated Press article, a spokesman for the California State Department of Health Services said Dr Babiera's permanent record 'contained a number of notations by Community Hospital staff indicating they were unable to reach him in emergencies'. In the same article, Riverside County Deputy Chief Coroner Carl Smith said: 'We would like to talk to him, but we can't force him to talk to us. We can't do anything until we find out what the people died of.' It was certainly seen as odd, maybe a little self-serving that the doctor was reluctant to cooperate.

Regardless, the investigators pressed on and the autopsies of two exhumed patients who died at the Perris hospital showed lethal doses of lidocaine, which is a local anaesthetic and antiarrhythmic drug. A police search of Diaz's house in May 1981 turned up two vials of lidocaine and a half-filled vial of morphine. Diaz explained that he must've put these drugs in his uniform pocket during an emergency and simply forgot to return them.

It wasn't until August 1981 that officials confirmed toxicology results from the autopsies of nine other patients showed that their deaths were due to lidocaine overdoses. Lidocaine is a local anaesthetic that works by blocking nerve signals in the body and creating a numbing effect.

'We are not talking about a therapeutic misadventure,' Deputy District Attorney Patrick Magers commented in a later interview with *The Press-Enterprise* newspaper (11 August 2010). 'We are talking about a huge amount of lidocaine – 1000 to 2000 milligrams. The average dose is 100 milligrams. So the victims received one injection that was 10 to 20 times higher than any injection should have been.'

The Assistant District Attorney Thomas Hollenhorst told the media the reasons for the deaths were now the focus for the investigation.

'Lidocaine doesn't fall out of the sky,' Hollenhorst said. 'Somebody had to administer it.'

Diaz was arrested on 23 November 1981 and held without bail. He requested a bench trial, where there is no jury and the judge decides the facts. His trial finally began in October 1983.

Diaz's nurse colleague Lois Cheville gave a tearful testimony that the accused serial killer always carried around a filled syringe in his pocket during his shift. Ms Cheville had worked with Diaz at Community Hospital of the Valleys in 1981 during the time when five of the patients he stood accused of murdering had died.

'The first time I saw it, I asked him about it because I don't believe nurses should put drugs in their pockets,' Ms Cheville told the court on 7 December 1983.

The Associated Press reported that Ms Cheville said the box in Diaz's pocket contained a packaged syringe filled with lidocaine. She said Diaz told her he carried it to always be prepared for an event where the drug might need to be used.

Ms Cheville said she never actually saw Diaz injecting any patients with the lidocaine but she witnessed the deaths of four of the patients whom Diaz was alleged to have murdered, and was asked to describe what she saw.

She said that these patients suffered convulsions that were unlike anything she had seen before in her 38 years of nursing. Ms Cheville told the court that the fits were not, in her opinion, consistent with an epilepsy convulsion and that the patients flailed their arms and arched their backs as their bodies stiffened.

When two patients died during one shift on 14 April 1981, Ms Cheville said she could no longer work at the hospital and handed in her resignation.

'After I finished the bookwork and the charts, I went to the superintendent of nurses and said I was leaving and not coming back,' Ms Cheville testified. 'I could not work there another five minutes. There were too many deaths. I never worked in a place where there were so many deaths.'

Another nurse Donna Macdonald testified that she had witnessed Diaz inject a patient's IV just before the patient died. Ms Macdonald said Diaz had also asked her to part-inject a syringe into the IV of another patient Henry Castro (who later died) but she had injected it into the bed instead.

Deputy District Attorney Patrick Magers put to the court that Diaz was the only link between the two hospitals' ICUs at the time of the patients' deaths.

There was never any real motive established for the crimes and prosecutor Mr Magers said the motive was mysterious in that Diaz's crimes were not the kind you'd typically see for a motive such as financial gain or revenge.

At the end of the five-month trial Diaz was found guilty of the murders of 12 patients, although he was suspected to have been involved in the deaths of as many as 48 patients.

After the verdict was announced, Mr Magers said the prosecution team felt justice was served and that the state would seek the death penalty for Diaz. 'How many lives can you take without facing the penalty of losing your own? He [Diaz] was placed in a position of trust, and violated it in the most appalling way.'

Diaz was one of 13 children, had been married twice and had five children. However, at his sentencing not a single character witness came forward. His second wife Martha, with whom he had four children, stopped visiting him in prison in August 1982.

On 11 April 1984, Diaz was sentenced to die in the gas chamber at the notorious San Quentin prison.

His lawyer, deputy public defender Michael Lewis said the decision 'didn't make my day'.

Diaz took an appeal against his conviction all the way to the California High Court but on 29 August 1992, the court justices upheld the death sentence six to one. The *Los Angeles Times* reported that the justices rejected Diaz's claims that there was insufficient evidence to prove that he was a murderer.

'Considered in its entirety, the evidence pointed unerringly to the defendant as the killer,' Justice Joyce L Kennard said.

Time moves slowly on death row and Diaz died aged 72 of natural causes on 11 August 2010 before he could face the lethal injection. (In 1994 the gas chamber was ruled 'cruel and unusual punishment' and unconstitutional. Lethal injection became the sole the method of execution at San Quentin). Diaz had experienced poor health and illness for many years and died in a hospital near the prison.

On Diaz's death, *The Press-Enterprise* newspaper interviewed the district attorney in the case – and by then a retired superior court judge – Patrick Magers.

'I cross-examined him for two days at trial and he denied any wrongdoing. He testified he gave the proper medication to his patients and had no explanation of how or why they had massive doses of lidocaine injected into their systems,' Magers said.

Diaz's case left another legacy besides horror and pain for the families of his victims. The case resulted in a major First Amendment decision by the Supreme Court.

California newspaper publisher Riverside Press-Enterprise challenged the ruling by the California court to make Diaz's 41-day preliminary hearing closed to the public after its reporters were barred from the courtroom. Diaz's defence had actually requested that his hearing be closed to the public and transcripts of the secret hearing were sealed for many months until his conviction. On 30 June 1986, in response to the *Riverside Press-Enterprise's* challenge, the Supreme Court of the United States in Washington ruled that the public had a constitutional right to attend pre-trial hearings in criminal cases over the objections of defendants.

Dr John Bodkin Adams

- The Luck of the Irish -

He is known as the serial killer who got away with it.

The case of Dr John Bodkin Adams was a worldwide sensation in the 1950s. The portly general practitioner lived and worked in the south-coast English seaside town Eastbourne and he had a reputation for being a particularly attentive doctor, especially to elderly wealthy widows.

As a young man from County Antrim, Northern Ireland, Adams answered an ad to join a firm of Christian GPs in Eastbourne, England, in 1922. He did not come with the best of skills having just scraped through his medical degree. But Adams was a deeply religious man and many believe it was this facade of respectability and devoutness that allowed him to go unchecked for almost 30 years, 'relieving' wealthy widows of their pain and their money.

Adams went into practice on his own, and lived with his mother and cousin. In 1929, when he was 30 years old, he purchased a Victorian villa called Kent Lodge for £3000. He borrowed money from a patient to pay for the villa as well as contributing some of his own savings to renovate the building. He furnished his consulting room with a chaise longue and had a steady supply of his favourite treat – violet cream chocolates delivered from Old Bond Street, London.

The doctor was in the house.

He also graduated from riding a scooter around town to a chauffeured limousine. In fact, Adams had a practice of referring his wealthy widow clients to London consultants, even accompanying them to the city in his Rolls Royce.

Adams was known to be on call day and night for his devoted patient base, mainly the lonely and vulnerable older women of area. Gossip swirled for many years about the doctor's treatment and bedside manner. He adopted some outdated practices, including hot water treatment for aches and pains, which involved sitting on a bucket of steaming water, and he liked to strongly suggest to his patients that he take power of attorney over their affairs. He even suggested to one woman who was hit in the eye with a tennis ball that she simply could not sign cheques anymore and that he could perform that task for her.

Adams received money from more than 300 wills and was left property, jewels, silverware and the luxury cars he so loved. The sums were significant for the time. In 1936 he was left £7000 by one Eastbourne widow. The relatives contested the will but Adams won in court and pocketed the money, which would be equivalent to more than £300,000 today.

How did this happen? Adams would tell his patients that rather than paying his bill, which would be taxed, the more sensible approach was for them to leave him a little something in their wills and this would not be taxed. If the patient had no living relatives, Adams encouraged them to leave their money to charity, but if they left the money to him, he would make sure the cash went directly to the benevolent causes. There were so many scams about, Adams would warn his widow patients, and it would be better to leave it in the hands of someone they trusted...like him.

Adams was the target of much professional jealousy and gossip over cups of tea in Eastbourne cafes and front sitting rooms. If you had made out a will to Dr Adams, you were not long for this earth.

It was the death in 1950 of 81-year-old Edith Morrell, the widow of a wealthy food importer, that Adams would eventually be taken to court over. Her death was famously known as the 'murder without a body' because her body was cremated, at Dr Adams's insistence.

Mrs Morrell was a very temperamental woman who had become dependent on pain medication, including morphine, after a stroke in 1948. It was the prosecution's case during the trial that Dr Adams made Mrs Morrell hopelessly addicted to the drugs and would dominate her by controlling the supply. Mrs Morrell made several wills between 1946 and 1950 and one version bequeathed a Rolls Royce, a chest of silver cutlery and an Elizabethan Court cupboard to Adams. From her cliff-top mansion in Eastbourne, Mrs Morrell wrote a codicil to her final will on 13 September 1950 that cut the doctor out completely. Hubert Sogno, who was Mrs Morrell's lawyer and made out her final will, appeared in court and said the doctor had made an appointment to see him personally.

'Adams said Mrs Morrell had promised many months previously that she would give him her Rolls Royce car in her will. He said she had forgotten to include him,' Mr Sogno said.

On her death, Dr Adams did get the Rolls Royce and silver cutlery, but it was thanks to the benevolence of Mrs Morrell's son Arthur who was the recipient of her estate.

In 1956, detectives investigated the deaths of around 400 wealthy women in Eastbourne who had been treated by Adams over the years. The investigations were initiated by the contents of anonymous letters to the police about the conduct of Dr John Bodkin Adams. Detectives were convinced Adams was responsible for many of these deaths – at least 163 – and financial gain was the motive.

'Easing the passing of a dying person is surely not all that wicked,' Adams told detectives making inquiries into the death of Mrs Morrell.

'She wanted to die, that cannot be murder.'

In August 1956, a coroner's jury found that one widow in particular, Gertrude Hullett, had died by suicide. Mrs Hullett's husband had left Adams £500 in his will, which would be worth over £20,000 today. A pathologist had discovered 20 barbiturate tablets in her stomach after her 23 July death. According to Adams, Mrs Hullett had become increasingly depressed since her husband's death and had hoarded the barbiturate tablets he had prescribed for her to take on holiday. However, police believed that Adams had murdered her and they were suspicious about her husband's death as well. Adams had treated the widow in the wake of her much older husband's death from apparent complications from bowel surgery. Adams admitted he had been given a cheque for £1000 by Mrs Hullett, who had been left almost £100,000 by her husband when he died in march 1956. In fact, Mrs Hullett died *the day after* she gave Adams the generous cheque. When Adams cashed the cheque on the day he received it, the bank clerk queried why Mrs Hullett's signature seemed so feint and illegible. Adams explained that the woman was very sick. Mrs Hullett had also left the doctor a Rolls Royce in her will.

Adams breathed a sigh of relief when the coroner's verdict on Mrs Hullett was announced.

'This should clear up all those malicious rumours,' Adams told reporters outside the court. 'Scotland Yard have assured me no allegations have been made against me.'

Adams was arrested on 25 November 1956 for the murder of Mrs Morrell. At Christmastime that year, detectives had the unenviable task of accompanying gravediggers to exhume the bodies of some of the elderly people that Dr Adams was suspected of murdering.

London Detective Superintendent Herbert (Bert) Hannam was the lead investigator tasked to ploughing through piles of wills, documents and deeds of hundreds of deceased wealthy Eastbourne residents from the previous 20 years.

People around the world were intrigued by the case. The setting of Eastbourne, was so quaint and, well, quintessentially English. It was often remarked in newspaper reports that even Agatha Christie couldn't have dreamt up a more perfect setting for an English murder mystery.

In his syndicated news feature 'The Strange Case of Dr John Bodkin Adams and the Wealthy Widows of Eastbourne', Newspaper Enterprise Association correspondent Tom A Cullen wrote that Eastbourne was the kind of town 'that hangs pots of pink geraniums on its railway station'.

'It [Eastbourne] looks down its aristocratic nose at noisy Brighton, where the London cockneys come to eat whelks and winkles and jellied eel, and to buy vulgar postcards,' Cullen wrote in the January 1957 article. And there was further intriguing detail from the journalist who travelled to the genteel town to discover more:

Certainly no writer could have dreamed up a more unlikely killer than short, bald, bespectacled Dr Adams, with his celluloid collars, who has been the town's leading physician for 33 years. And not only physician. Dr Adams, a 57-year-old Ulster-born bachelor, was president of the Eastbourne Y.M.C.A. He taught Sunday school. And he was the Chief Constable's personal physician...

The life of Detective Bert Hannam also proved great newspaper fodder. Detective Superintendent Hannam was quite the chef and relaxed by making pastries and cakes. He actually started his career as a pastry chef in the 1930s, before he joined the Metropolitan Police. 'On weekends he is to be found in the kitchen of his ground floor apartment at Willesden icing a cake or putting the finishing touches to a chocolate éclair,' Cullen wrote.

Detective Hannam (described by one reporter as 'tall, poker faced, tailored by Bond Street') was already somewhat of a public identity, having used his meticulous investigation methods to solve the murder of two teenage girls in Richmond in 1953.

On 31 May, Barbara Songhurst, 16 and Christine Reed, 18, had been out on their bicycles on the Thames towpath but failed to return home to Teddington in Middlesex. Barbara's body was found the next day, the eve of Queen Elizabeth II's coronation, and Christine's almost one week later. Both girls had been beaten, raped and stabbed. Alfred Whiteway, 22, was arrested and stood trial for the crime. Whiteway was hanged for the murders at Wandsworth Prison on 22 December 1953.

During Adams's January 1957 preliminary hearings, there was much damning testimony against the doctor. Nurse Caroline Randall said she told Dr Adams to stop giving heroin to Mrs Morrell when it became clear she was in the grip of addiction.

Two other nurses said that Dr Adams was secretive about the injections he would administer to his patients. The nurse said she and her colleagues, who had attended to Mrs Morrell over the years since her stroke, were never allowed in the room when Dr Adams was with the elderly woman. It seemed that Adams was dosing the poor woman with heavier and heavier measures of the drugs until she died.

Detective Hannam told magistrates at the preliminary hearing about Adams' suspicious behaviour when he was arrested.

A United Press syndicated article reported on 22 January 1957 that the detective said Adams went to a cupboard in his surgery and 'took out two objects which he put into his pocket'.

He relayed the conversation he had with Adams that day.

'You've put something in your pocket,' Detective Hannam said to Adams.

'No, I've got nothing,' Adams replied.

The report said: 'The detective then testified he then moved close to the doctor demanding "what was it?" and Adams then took out of his pocket two bottles of morphine.'

The trial was heard at London's Old Bailey and ran for 17 days, which at the time was the longest ever murder trial in English history. During the trial, Adams did not take the stand in his own defence. The reason for this was said to be down to Adams' barrister fearing that his client, who was pompous and liked the sound of his own voice, would make his defence job harder.

A 19 March 1957 report from AAP-Reuters of the first day of trial summed up the atmosphere of the Old Bailey and the doctor's demeanour. 'The portly, blue-suited doctor hurried up the stairs from the cells into the large dock. He looked straight ahead at the bewigged and red-robed figure of the judge while the charge was being read. Then he said, in a loud, clear voice, "I am not guilty, my lord".'

The first witness for the defence, a Harley Street physician Dr John Harman, provided a suitable dose of drama for the courtroom when he staged a mock collapse to show what a spinal convulsion brought on by a morphine overdose would look like.

'Slowly raising his arms, he bent over backwards till he disappeared from the view of the eyes staring at him in the hushed court,' AAP-Reuter reported on 4 April 1957.

Dr Harman's opinion on the medical cause of Mrs Morrell's death was that it could have simply been heart failure.

'In old ladies over 80 who have had strokes and arteriosclerosis, one does not regard it as a question so much of explaining; the cause of death. One knows they just die. It is very difficult to know for certain why they die. The immediate cause of death might well have come from the heart – coronary thrombosis,' Dr Harman said.

Two hundred journalists from all over Britain and the world were in attendance. There were daily updates in newspapers around the world that were voraciously read by people intrigued by the case. Director Alfred Hitchcock had reportedly become fascinated by the case too. It took the jury of 10 men and two women just 44 minutes to acquit the doctor of murder. The other secret indictment of the murder of Gertrude Hullett was also dropped.

'When the verdict was announced, he remained motionless, staring ahead at the judge. The only sign of emotion was a deep flush...' United Press International reported on 9 April 1957. The story 'Jury acquits Dr Adams' was syndicated in newspapers across the world.

After his acquittal, Adams successfully sued several London newspapers, including the *Daily Mail*.

However, Adams sold his story to *The Express* for £10,000. A photo taken by the newspaper of Adams shows him looking jolly, smartly dressed (as ever) in one of his Savile Row suits with his pudgy fingers and carving into a celebratory roast bird, with a bottle of Chianti on the table. Strangely, Adams never used the cash from the newspaper exclusive and it was found, still in the same envelope, in a safety deposit box after his death.

A legal committee was set up in June 1957 in the wake of Adams's acquittal. The committee recommended that newspapers should not be allowed to report preliminary hearings at which it is decided whether or not an accused person should go for trial.

Despite being found not guilty, Adams's career was in ruin. The Eastbourne Medical Society did not welcome him anymore and the General Medical Council then struck him off. This was due to him being fined for forgeries in relation to The Cremation Act and the prescription of drugs.

In 1961, Adams was reinstated to the General Medical Council and he was able to practice medicine again. However, rumour and innuendo followed him for the rest of his life. Adams became a recluse.

Consultant gynaecologist Brian Valentine, 59, who bought Adams' Kent Lodge for £90,000 in 1984, told *The Telegraph* in a 2001 interview that the property was in ruin when its infamous owner died.

'Fear and anxiety haunted Adams for the rest of his life,' Mr Valentine said.

Adams, frightened that someone might firebomb the house, stepped up security and screwed the sash windows shut and fitted fire extinguishers on every landing.

Adams died in 1983 after falling and breaking his hip. He was 84.

In a twist that was stranger than any fiction a crime writer could dream up, a reclusive con artist called Sybil Dreda-Owen challenged Adams' will.

Dreda-Owen made a fortune challenging the wills of rich and famous men. She won £53,000 from Adams' will.

Working in cahoots with her daughter Barbara Hatje, Dreda-Owen owned homes in London, Sussex and Switzerland. The first will she challenged was that of the author LP Hartley, who wrote *The Go-Between*, (later made into a film starring Julie Christie) who died in 1972 at age 76. The life and times of Dreda-Owen were revealed in 1995 by *The Sunday Times* when she was embroiled in a fourth inheritance dispute. In the case of Hartley's will, Dreda-Owen claimed the author, who was openly gay, fathered her daughter Barbara. She reputedly won a settlement of £377,000 from his estate.

British television's Channel 4 screened a documentary for its series *Cutting Edge* called 'Inheritance' in 1996 and it revealed some startling information about the elderly woman dubbed the 'queen of wills'. Disturbingly, it was discovered that Dreda-Owen was a con artist who had plied her trade for more than 40 years. In 1955, a private detective who was investigating a series of 'lonely hearts' scams on wealthy, elderly men, handed his research to Scotland Yard. One of the names included in the dossier was that of Ms Dreda-Owen.

The *Sunday Times* interviewed one of the victims of Dreda-Owens, who was by now aged in her early 70s. Peter Ainley was expecting to share the inheritance of his uncle Walter Joslin, who died in 1991 aged 83, with the old man's local church. Mr Joslin, a retired civil servant, was extremely frail and had very poor eyesight in the years before his death. Dreda-Owen befriended the man and on his death, produced a will, allegedly written by Mr Joslin, which left his money and London home to her daughter Barbara. This will was dated three months before Joslin's death and the man's solicitor knew nothing of its existence. There had been a will with Mr Joslin's solicitor that his family and church assumed was the man's final wish. Mr Ainley and the church did not challenge Ms Dreda-Owen because of the prohibitive legal costs they faced if they lost the court action. Ms Dreda Owen's daughter Barbara Hatje received most of Mr Joslin's £400,000 estate.

The newspaper also discovered two witnesses who Ms Dreda-Owen persuaded to sign the will. The pair, Andrew Scott-Stokes and Randa Hawa, said they were uneasy about what they had done (Ms Hawa said on camera what Ms Dreda-Owen did to her was 'emotional blackmail'), although they had no evidence that Mr Joslin had been forced into making the new will that left everything to Dreda-Owen and her daughter.

Ms Hawa, who worked in a bookshop near Ms Dreda-Owen's London home, told the Channel 4 documentary that she had been offered financial assistance for costs should she have to go to court to substantiate the woman's story. Mr Scott-Stokes, who worked in an art shop in Hampstead, said he had been promised he could inherit Mr Joslin's former home.

Mr Ainley, who was also interviewed for the documentary, said, 'This woman has made a profession over the years challenging wills. Conveniently, in all cases, the only men who could tell the truth about exactly what happened are dead.'

Adams remains a fascinating figure of notoriety. When the shocking case of Dr Harold Shipman hit the headlines, Dr John Bodkin Adams' name was often mentioned. Shipman, a general practitioner in England, killed at least 300 of his patients. Shipman was convicted of 15 murders and became known worldwide as one of the most prolific serial killers ever.

Shipman was reportedly intrigued by John Bodkin Adams and eerily had a link with the controversial doctor. *The Sun* reported on 1 February 2000 that the father-in-law of Dr Michael Grieve, a senior partner of Shipman's at a GP practice where he worked during the mid-1970s, had been a patient of Adams. The newspaper revealed in its article 'Echoes of Bodkin Adams' that Dr Grieve had told Shipman that his father-in-law's condition had not improved after he started to be seen by the Eastbourne doctor. However, when Dr Grieve took over the treatment himself, his father-in-law made a complete recovery. 'I never knew whether Bodkin Adams was poisoning him,' Dr Grieve said.

So, was Adams helping the suffering of his elderly patients or actually murdering them for avarice?

If he was one of Britain's worst serial killers, Dr John Bodkin Adams was also one of the luckiest men to have, literally, got away with murder.

Kimberly Saenz

- The Bleach Killer -

Her murder weapon was bleach and the victims had no idea that instead of life-saving care, they were being poisoned at the hands of their nurse.

Nurse Kimberly Saenz worked at the private DaVita Kidney Care dialysis clinic in the East Texas town of Lufkin. Lufkin is in Angelina County and is surrounded by the natural beauty of two state forests and large reservoir Lake Sam Rayburn. Founded in 1882, the town was built upon the fortunes of the timber industry and is now home to almost 40,000 people.

DaVita Kidney Care is a division of the California-based DaVita Inc., and has more than 2000 dialysis centres around the United States and overseas. On its corporate website, it is explained that *da vita* is Italian for 'giving life' but unfortunately for the patients at the Luftkin clinic, one of their nurses was of a mind to kill instead.

Kimberly Saenz, a licensed vocational nurse, was the mother of two young children, attended church and was, by many accounts, a well-liked and reliable employee who had worked at the dialysis centre for eight months leading up to April 2008. However, appearances can be deceptive, and they were with Kimberly Saenz. April would prove to be a deadly month for the clinic, with ambulances called out 30 times that month. Four people died and seven underwent emergency treatments for heart problems. According to the Texas Department of Health Services there had been just two calls to emergency services during the previous 15 months.

An anonymous letter from a senior health official to the Texas Department of Health Services in April 2008 implored them to investigate the abnormally high call for paramedics to the dialysis clinic. Investigators arrived to take a look at the claims and a review of clinic records found that Saenz was on duty for 84 per cent of instances where patients had a cardiac arrest or complained of chest pains.

Saenz and her husband Mark were experiencing troubles in their marriage and this escalated in 2007 when he filed for divorce.

Saenz was dependent on prescription drugs and had been fired from several healthcare jobs for being intoxicated and stealing medication. In 2005, one healthcare facility actually filed charges against her for stealing the drug Demerol (a narcotic pain medication). However, Saenz managed to keep these charges a secret and lied on her job applications, and was able to find employment again.

Eventually though, everything seemed to catch up with Saenz and she became careless. On 28 April 2008, at the clinic, witnesses saw her inject what they believed to be bleach into the dialysis lines of two patients, Marva Rhone and Carolyn Risinger. Both patients survived Saenz's actions, but she lost her job at DaVita that day and the clinic voluntarily closed its doors to improve its practices and protocols.

The following evening, 29 April 2008, the local police were called to Mark Saenz's address. Lufkin police officer Bradley Baker attended the call and found Saenz banging on the door. She appeared glassy-eyed and unable to communicate. Baker issued a criminal trespass warrant against Saenz and arrested her for public intoxication. Saenz spent the night in the lock-up and a judge issued a temporary restraining order against her on behalf of Mark Saenz, who feared she was dangerous.

Saenz was arrested in May 2008 by the Lufkin police and charged with two counts of aggravated assault for allegedly injecting bleach into the dialysis lines of the two patients. At the same time, the Texas Board of Nursing suspended her nursing licence.

She gave evidence at an Angelina County grand jury in early 2009.

'I feel so railroaded. There's this big company, and they need to get out of it, so they need a scapegoat,' Saenz said. 'I would never inject bleach into a patient. I've been trying to rack my brain to see where they would come up with this.'

Saenz claimed that as more patients on dialysis became ill and died, she and her co-workers became concerned. Saenz tried to explain the fact that investigators had found search terms on her home computer that related to information on bleach poisoning.

'I don't know where it came from, but someone said, "Are we getting all the bleach out of the lines?" That stuck in my head,' Saenz told the grand jury. 'There was bleach everywhere, but how was it getting in the lines? We were trying to figure it out, and it was really kind of scary.'

On 2 April 2009, the grand jury indicted Saenz for one count of capital murder and five counts of aggravated assault but her case did not go to trial until 2012. Between her arrest and the trial, Saenz was not under any bail conditions.

The alleged murder victims were Clara Strange, Thelma Metcalf, Opal Few, Garlin Kelley and Cora Bryant.

The trial, held in Angelina County, attracted media from all over the country and the crime was dissected on live television by the likes of Nancy Grace – former prosecutor and now outspoken crime and legal commentator and television host – each night.

Local newspaper *Lufkin Daily News* provided the most in-depth coverage to the community which had been shocked by the allegations against Saenz.

Saenz's defence team claimed that their client was a scapegoat for sloppy and dangerous practices by the DaVita clinic. The investigation in the deaths had revealed that there were some practices at DaVita that did not meet certain state-required standards.

Linda Hall was one of the witnesses who observed Saenz draw up bleach from a cleaning bucket and then inject it into the two patients' dialysis lines. Ms Hall was the first witness for the prosecution team and she described Saenz as 'fidgety' as she injected the bleach into Marva Rhone and Carolyn Risinger.

'I said, "Lord, what is she doing?" She walked to Ms Rhone's IV, looked around and then went to the port hole, pushed it in there and stepped back,' Ms Hall recalled to the court.

Saenz's defence called nine witnesses, who spoke of the accused's devotion to her work, her friends and her two children's schoolwork and athletics.

Among those was Peggy Wells, a long-time friend of Saenz.

'I've known her for 33 years,' Wells told the court.

'I've known her since kindergarten. She's been a friend all my life. She came to my house the Halloween after she was arrested. I was not worried about her being there.'

Saenz was found guilty of murder on 2 April 2012. She also received three 20-year terms for aggravated assault in the cases of five other patients.

The death penalty was a distinct possibility for the mother-of-two.

Clyde Herrington, Angelina County District Attorney, was a well-known figure in East Texas. Born in Lufkin, he had worked at the District Attorney's office for 23 years.

Mr Herrington painted a picture to the jurors of Saenz as a deceitful woman, not a scapegoat as her defence wanted them to believe. He told the jury to remember that Saenz was found with drugs stolen while she was working as a hospital nurse and tried to fake a urine test to evade detection.

He also showed them pictures of the victims on a large screen in the courtroom.

'I know you'll reach a verdict that's just and in accordance with the law.

'The victims in this case were patients that went in for medical treatment to try to prolong their lives and the only thing they did wrong was trust the defendant,' Mr Herrington said.

Mr Herrington believed that there were more victims than the indicted cases. Lufkin Police detectives could only obtain medical waste from two weeks prior to 28 April 2008, so there wasn't enough evidence to definitively link Saenz to the other incidents.

Wanda Hollingsworth, who lost her mother, told KYTX CBS W19 news reporter Field Sutton that she hoped Saenz would get the death penalty. It was a sentiment echoed by Marie Bradley, one of three of

Saenz's victims who survived the lethal bleach injection. 'She shot us up with stuff that shouldn't have been in our bodies, so …' Ms Bradley said in an interview with Sutton.

Ms Hollingsworth, who is a nurse herself, described Saenz as a 'psychopathic killer' who had disgraced her family and the medical field.

'She's stripped so much away from so many people,' Ms Hollingsworth said.

Saenz escaped the death penalty and was sentenced to life in prison.

Dezmond Scott, grandson of victim Cora Bryant, told assembled media outside the courtroom, 'My heart goes out to Kimberly Saenz's family, you know, she's still a human being, I feel sorry for her but we have relief now, we can finally put this behind us.'

Denver-based company DaVita reopened the Lufkin clinic two months after it was closed in the wake of the deaths and Saenz's arrest. The business had worked hard to improve operations to the level that was required by the Texas Department of Health and the Center for Disease Control.

'We're grateful justice has prevailed,' DaVita spokesman Vince Hancock said.

'We hope the healing can finally start to occur for families of victims and for our teammates who also have been victimised by the murderous acts of Kimberly Saenz.'

As with most causes these days, social media is an effective way for people to rally support for their cause. There is a Facebook page dedicated to proving Saenz's innocence called 'Release Kim'. At the time of writing, the last activity on the page was 12 July 2013. The profile picture shows a much younger Saenz with, presumably, one of her children when they were very young.

One man, David Stua, has made it his mission to prove that Saenz is innocent and has bombarded the Angelina County and Cities Health District and the Lufkin Police Department with requests for open records. In a July 2013 interview with an East Texas ABC affiliate television station, Mr Stua, who describes himself as a public information activist, estimated that he made so many requests that the departments would have to source 18,000 documents. But Lufkin County Police Chief Scott Marcotte said that Mr Stua's requests would keep the police from doing what they are supposed to do: protect citizens.

Mr Stua said, 'I'm not trying to cause the city or the health district any problems with their primary functions, although responding to an open records request is a critical responsibility of theirs as well.'

Mr Stua wanted the records to prove his theory that prescription drugs caused the deaths of five patients, not the bleach-filled injections that Saenz was found guilty of administering to them.

'Kimberly Saenz is innocent. She did not commit these murders,' said Mr Stua.

Mr Stua has proved challenging for the local public offices. In April 2012, board members for the Angelina County and Cities Health District were forced to raise the district's legal budget by US$58,000, mostly to handle the volume of open records requests submitted by Mr Stua.

Lufkin District Attorney Jimmy Cassels told the board that David Stua's numerous Freedom of Information Act requests were responsible for the majority of a 175 per cent overrun in the original legal fees budget of US$14,000.

Angelina County District Attorney Clyde Herrington retired from the DA's office in December 2012. Herrington told television station KTRE that the Saenz prosecution was his toughest case.

'That was probably the longest, most complicated case I've ever handled,' Herrington said. 'As DA you get to prosecute folks that are dangerous and hurt people and you also get to try and help people. A lot of folks make mistakes and they're not evil and they need a hand up.'

Herrington considered Saenz to be in the 'dangerous' category.

In early 2014, the Fourth Texas Court of Appeals, based in San Antonio determined that Saenz was properly convicted and sentenced. Her lawyers then took the case to the Court of Criminal Appeals.

In 2016 The Supreme Court denied Saenz's appeal.

Donald Harvey

- The 'Sweet Child' -

From all accounts, Donald Harvey was a neat, smart and well-mannered little boy.

As a child, Harvey – known then as Donnie – was raised in the small town of Booneville, Kentucky. So how did this quiet, sweet-natured boy become one of America's worst serial killers by the age of 35?

According to forensic psychology experts and police, the answers likely lie in events from Harvey's childhood. But according to people who knew Harvey as a boy and his family, there was no sign that he would turn to evil deeds.

In a 30 August 1987 article, *Daily News* (the newspaper for Bowling Green, Kentucky) printed an Associated Press report that quoted Harvey's mother Goldie Harvey McKinney, schoolteachers and old neighbours from Booneville saying they could not match Harvey the alleged serial killer with the boy they knew. Classmates from the Sturgeon School, where Harvey started in 1958, recalled him as one of the nicest boys in school.

'People kind of called him a sissy, you know, he didn't get fighting mad. He just went about his business,' said Danny Day, who went to school with Harvey.

Teacher Lena Gabbard remembered Harvey as a 'beautiful child' with curly hair, brown eyes and always smiling. Ms Gabbard said Harvey was intelligent and was reading at a level much higher than his classmates at Oswald County Elementary School.

'He wanted always to do what the teacher wanted and he was helpful,' Ms Gabbard said.

And Harvey came from what Ms Gabbard recalled was 'a good home'.

'She [Harvey's mother Goldie Harvey McKinney] put so much into presenting her child at school in the very best appearances that she could. Whenever Goldie was needed at the school, she was always there to help. Whenever there was a PTA meeting, whenever there was a Christmas play, Goldie would be there,' Ms Gabbard said.

However, it later emerged that from the age of four, Harvey was sexually abused for several years by his mother's half-brother and then also by a teenage neighbour.

Harvey dropped out of school unexpectedly in his freshman year, aged 14. He managed to continue his studies by correspondence and got his General Educational Development (GED) qualification, equivalent to a high school diploma and a prerequisite for most entry-level jobs.

As a teenager, Harvey's sexual orientation was towards males and he began his first consensual relationships from the age of 16.

For unknown reasons, following the completion of his GED, Harvey relocated to Cincinnati, Ohio and obtained work in a factory.

Harvey's life as a serial killer began when he was 18. It was 1970 and Harvey was working as an orderly at Marymount Hospital in London, Kentucky. It was his first job in healthcare. In London KY, Harvey was staying with June White and her son Kyle, a local hairdresser and businessman. She worked in the hospital office and her husband was an orderly there, and Harvey got his job through Mrs White.

Forensic psychologists and expert detectives often say that a serial killer's first victim is the most significant. For Donald Harvey, his first (known) murder was on 31 May 1970 when he smothered an elderly male patient, 88, with a plastic sheet and pillow.

In the 10-month period Harvey worked at the hospital he killed more than a dozen patients. Harvey's modus operandi was all over the place.

There was no consistent motivation for his murders – he later claimed some were 'mercy' killings. But as investigators would eventually discover, Harvey killed for many reasons, and not many people bought his 'angel of mercy' excuse.

Sometimes Harvey's victims died quickly, sometimes slowly and in an excruciatingly cruel manner. On 31 May 1970, Harvey murdered James Tyree, 69, after inserting a wrong-sized catheter. Mr Tyree screamed out in pain and told Harvey to take the catheter out. Realising his mistake, Harvey held the patient down until he vomited blood and died. Harvey admitted later that he was inexperienced in caring for patients when he started work at the hospital.

On 22 June 1970, Harvey cut off the oxygen supply to 42-year-old Elizabeth Wyatt, a patient with terminal cancer, and she died quickly. 'I never meant to kill her,' Harvey told reporters later, after his conviction for the killing of nine people at Marymount Hospital. 'But days of seeing her suffer and having to force feed her...that was no way to live.'

Another case was the death of John V Combs, in January 1971. Mr Combs was in poor health anyway so while his family was not suspicious when he died they were disturbed at the horrible way it had happened.

'Blood from his mouth and nose had spurted all over the bed and the wall and everything,' his daughter Dorothy Martin said.

Ms Martin said she had wondered why an orderly (she could not confirm that it was Harvey) had spent time with her dad just before he died.

'About 45 minutes before he died, there was an orderly came into the room. He pulled the curtain around my father's bed.'

At the time of Ms Martin's comments in 1987, officials were still going through the painstaking process of identifying Harvey's victims, and Mr Combs's family was waiting to hear if their father had been murdered. It was later determined John V Combs had been killed by Harvey after being given a faulty oxygen mask.

Other deaths at Harvey's hand resulted from blatant disregard for instructions. One such example occurred on 10 July 1970, when Harvey turned patient Eugene McQueen, 43, onto his stomach, when he knew this was actually not allowed due to the patient's condition. Mr McQueen died from drowning in his own bodily fluids. Harvey, anxious to hide his actions, continued his 'duties' and bathed Mr McQueen even though he knew he was dead.

Authorities had a chance to halt Harvey's killing spree early – on 1 April 1971, the day after he ceased employment at the hospital, a drunk Harvey was arrested for burglary. He pleaded guilty to petty theft and was fined $50. During the police interview for the theft, Harvey was reported to have made comments that he had harmed patients at the hospital but this story was not followed up.

Following this, Harvey enlisted in the United States Air Force. However, Harvey was depressed and unstable and had taken at least two overdoses with over-the-counter cold medication. He was discharged from the air force after the suicide attempt resulted in his superiors finding out about his fragile mental state and his criminal record.

Harvey went on to work at Cardinal Hill Convalescent Hospital in Lexington, Kentucky in 1972–75; the VA (Veterans Administration) Hospital in Cincinnati, Ohio in 1975–85; and Daniel Drake Memorial Hospital, also in Cincinnati, from 1986 to the time of his arrest in June 1987. He continued to murder his patients at all three locations.

All throughout his adult years, Harvey's life was quite chaotic and there had been several cries for help including an incident in 1971 where he set fire to an empty apartment in the block where he lived. It was thought to be an unsuccessful suicide attempt.

Harvey had many relationships, which could be very turbulent. In 1980, he was dating a man called Doug Hill. This relationship became significant because Harvey slipped arsenic into Doug's ice cream one night in retaliation after a heated argument. Arsenic soon became Harvey's new weapon of destruction.

When Harvey laced his boyfriend's food with arsenic, it was the first time he had harmed someone outside a hospital setting. But it wouldn't be the last.

Harvey was often possessive and needy in his relationships. In 1980, he began seeing hairdresser Carl Hoeweler and anyone who got in the way of the couple was in danger.

Harvey was jealous of Carl's friendship with a woman named Diane Alexander and was worried she was trying to split them up. Harvey tried to infect Diane with hepatitis B by slipping a hepatitis serum, which he'd stolen from his workplace, into her drink. Diane became very sick and was hospitalised, but survived.

Next, Harvey started to give his lover small doses of arsenic-laced food after the pair had arguments and would then nurse Carl back to health. In those moments, Harvey held all the power.

In 1983, Harvey poisoned Carl's parents, Henry and Margaret, with arsenic. Mr Hoeweler Senior, 82, died a few days later from a stroke and kidney failure. (Carl Hoeweler died in 2015 aged 74.). Harvey also caused the death of Carl's brother-in-law Howard Vetter when he accidentally served him poisoned alcohol.

Being close to Donald Harvey was proving deadly. Harvey's neighbour Edgar Wilson was poisoned in 1985. Mr Wilson, 81, was actually a patient at the VA Hospital when Harvey put arsenic in the elderly man's stomach medication.

Harvey's ability to offend with ease was very much a symptom of administrative flaws that meant his murderous spree went unnoticed for years. While at the VA Hospital, Harvey was being investigated by an undercover police officer for the theft of hospital property. The officer saw Harvey slip a gun into his workbag. Also in the bag were stolen tissue samples and three books on the occult. Harvey was issued a fine for a weapons violation but was allowed to resign from the hospital and the matter was never revealed to his next – and last – employer, Daniel Drake Memorial Hospital.

The murder of 44-year-old John Powell on 7 March 1987 brought Harvey's shocking crimes to light. Mr Powell had suffered serious brain damage from a motorcycle accident seven months prior and under Ohio law at the time, all fatal victims of auto accidents had to be autopsied. This was to determine the exact cause of death for liability in any lawsuits. Harvey had killed Mr Powell with a dose of cyanide in his gastric feeding tube.

It so happened that the pathologist doing the autopsy had a particular talent for sniffing out cyanide. Deputy coroner Dr Lee Lehman was not only a doctor but he also had a PhD in chemistry. When he was a student at Indiana University he had often worked with cyanide in the laboratory and had come to know the subtle smell of the poison. Even some of his most experienced fellow pathologists may never have detected the presence of poison while doing the autopsy on Mr Powell.

'I checked the lungs and found a bad pneumonia,' Dr Lehman explained at a press conference after Harvey was charged.

'I was just about ready to write it up that way but an autopsy requires that every organ of the body be opened and checked. When I opened the stomach, I smelled cyanide,' he said.

'You have to understand, we had no suspicion of foul play in Powell's death. A toxicological assessment is not a routine part of the autopsy. And without some giveaway of poisoning, a coroner is not expecting to find some toxins in the deceased.'

When authorities worked out Harvey was the last person to be in contact with Mr Powell, he was arrested. Police searched Harvey's apartment and found jars of cyanide and arsenic, as well as books on poisoning.

Dr Lehman was hailed as a hero in newspaper reports and was even dubbed 'the nose that saved Cincinnati' in the *Pittsburgh Post-Gazette* on 14 November 1987.

Roger D Smith, the then director of the Department of Pathology and Laboratory at the University of Cincinnati was one of several experts who said Donald Harvey was clear proof that hospitals needed to perform more autopsies. During the 1980s, autopsies done after deaths in US hospitals had dropped dramatically. In the 1970s, almost half the deaths in hospitals ended up being autopsied. But with improved technologies and hospital administrations trying to cut costs, autopsies were seen as a diagnostic tool that could be scaled back.

'Obviously, if hospitals did a lot of autopsies it would be a deterrent to people like Harvey, because they would be caught,' Dr Smith told reporter Robert White from Scripps Howard News Service for a 1987 article.

'Who knows? Maybe there are more Harveys around,' he said.

The news that Harvey had confessed to so many murders left his former co-workers shocked. By all accounts, Harvey was a well-liked and hard-working employee.

Harvey's boss for seven years at the VA Hospital's morgue, Gaza Parmetier, said he could not say a bad word against his former worker.

'He was very nice, always liked by his co-workers. I'm shocked,' Mr Parmetier told a wire news service reporter.

Hamilton County prosecutor Arthur Ney Jr believed that without a confession, there might not be enough evidence to convince a jury of Harvey's guilt. Harvey was scared of receiving the death penalty, which was looking quite likely given the gravity of his crimes. Harvey ended up plea bargaining his way out of the death penalty by pleading guilty and saving the state a long and costly trial. He told his lawyers he had killed over 50 people during his 16 years as a nurse's aide.

'He's no mercy killer and he's not insane. He killed because he liked to kill,' Mr Ney Jr said.

'This man is sane, competent, but is a compulsive killer...he builds up tension in his body so he kills people.'

Mr Ney Jr said Harvey had a compulsion to kill like some people had 'a compulsion for malted milk or cold beer'.

Forensic psychiatrist Dr Emmanual Tanay testified before the grand jury and said that Harvey's compulsion to kill was a personality defect rather than a mental illness. Dr Tanay said Harvey's confessions to murder were most likely prompted by solid legal advice rather than 'a stricken conscience'.

But Harvey's mother believed her son had tricked the doctors into thinking he was sane. Mrs McKinney told the Cleveland *Plain Dealer* newspaper in August 1987 that her son had been hospitalised three times during the 1970s for psychological disturbances.

'He's sick,' she told the *Plain Dealer*. 'He's in a good mood now. In two months he's going to be off his rocker again.'

The sentences he received for the Marymount Hospital killings were to run concurrently with the 25 life terms he received for the murders in Cincinnati – 21 of them at Daniel Drake Memorial Hospital.

Judge Lewis Hopper, who presided over the sentencing of Harvey for the Marymount hospital murders, remarked that he had difficulty accepting that the nurse's aide's crimes were an act of mercy for suffering patients.

After the sentencing for the Marymount Hospital murders, the waiting media had access to the man who was now officially one of America's most prolific serial killers. Harvey spoke with candour that had the reporters writing furiously in their notebooks.

Chilling in his frankness, Harvey told the reporters that he believed there were more people like him working in hospitals around the United States.

'I think there's several Donald Harveys out there but with my story, they'll be more careful,' he said.

On 28 March 2017, Harvey was found badly beaten in his cell at Toledo Correctional Institution, Ohio. He died a few days later from massive head injuries.

A fellow inmate had bashed Harvey with the intention of killing the notorious prisoner.

The pair were housed in a protective custody unit of the prison.

Harold Shipman

- Dr Death -

I'm very conscious of coming across real evil ... there's evil here...

Father Denis Maher, Hyde, England, 2000

In the chilling realm of healthcare serial killers, British general practitioner Harold Frederick Shipman is among the worst of the worst for the sheer scale of his offences. Much detailed and compelling copy – books, feature articles, documentaries – has been produced about Shipman. Shipman's offences took place in working-class English towns and his place as a beloved family doctor firmly puts him in the class of killers who are the most baffling and dangerous. The writers of *Midsomer Murders* or the queen of crime Agatha Christie could not have dreamed up this story.

Shipman was a respected – almost revered – GP in the Northern England town Hyde for much of his medical career. However, far from nurturing his patients, from the early 1970s to 1998, Shipman was murdering those in his care. In January 2000, he was convicted of murdering 15 of his patients. His murder weapon was diamorphine (the medical name for heroin) – lethal doses of the drug are used for terminal stages of cancer for pain relief. The scale of his killing is far greater than his conviction indicated. Police and the Department of Health, who audited Shipman's mortality data, believe Shipman killed hundreds of patients during his career. *The Shipman Inquiry* was undertaken by the British Government following Shipman's arrest and trial, and the findings released in various stages.

Hyde is a working-class town of Greater Manchester, with a population of roughly 35,000. The town's history is intrinsically linked with industry – during the industrial revolution there were 40 working mills and a colliery. The town hall is both historically important and notorious for being the place where child killer Myra Hindley and her lover Ian Brady were interviewed over their depraved crimes. (The police station was located in the town hall as was the magistrates' court where Brady and Hindley had their first hearing.) The evil duo killed five children between 1963 and 1965 and buried four of the bodies on the desolate Saddleworth Moor. Brady was arrested on 7 October 1965 and Hindley four days later, at their Hyde home, where they also murdered their last victim.

Around 10 years after Brady and Hindley were arrested, Shipman, having moved with his young family to Hyde, is believed to have committed his first-known murder. However, it is thought he began killing much earlier than that.

The death of Kathleen Grundy, 81, in 1998 was the catalyst for the unravelling of Shipman's decades of casual and callous murder. Mrs Grundy, an active lady who volunteered for charities and was a former mayor of the town, was found dead in the chair of her living room. Shipman had been at the cottage just hours earlier to take a blood sample. There was a will that indicated Mrs Grundy left her entire estate, worth more than £386,000 to Shipman.

Two days before Mrs Grundy's death, a law firm in Hyde received a will purporting to be from her that bequeathed her estate to Shipman. The law firm had never done business with Mrs Grundy before.

Mrs Grundy's daughter Angela Woodruff, who was a solicitor, spent several weeks making her own investigations into the will, which she knew was a forgery. Ms Woodruff had a copy of her mother's will in her possession, and had done for many years. She had never heard of an updated will. The updated will was written sloppily and was not the neat, cohesive document her meticulous mother would have arranged. Later, police found the will had been cobbled together on a typewriter in Shipman's surgery and that his fingerprints were on the document.

Ms Woodruff drove to Hyde and spoke to the two people who were allegedly witnesses to this new will. Paul Spencer, who was one of the witnesses, was later interviewed for the documentary *Doctor Death*, directed and produced by Clive Entwistle and shown on Britain's Channel 5 on the evening that Shipman was found guilty of 15 murders.

Spencer recalled that he was in the crowded doctor's surgery when Shipman popped his head in and asked if two people would witness a document. Spencer and a woman, Claire Hutchinson, went in to the doctor's room and saw an elderly woman: Mrs Grundy.

Shipman handed Mr Spencer a folded-over piece of paper and told the young man where to sign it. As far as Mr Spencer knew, he was signing a medical document and not a will. He recalled that he couldn't see what was on the document because it was folded over, 'and being in a doctor's surgery I didn't dream of asking.'

In front of these two patients, Shipman asked Mrs Grundy if she was absolutely all right with the document, which already had her signature. She indicated 'yes'. However, as the documentary narrator Peter Lane explained, Mrs Grundy thought the document was simply an authorisation to take part in a medical questionnaire on ageing for Manchester University.

'It wasn't a case of *Look, she's not left me anything in her will,*' Ms Woodruff explained to BBC reporter Andrew Walker in a February 2001 interview. It was unbelievable that Mrs Grundy would have left this amount of money to her doctor.

There was also the request in the new will that stated Mrs Grundy wanted to be cremated. From previous conversations with her mother, Ms Woodruff was under the impression that this was not how her mother wanted her body to be dealt with after death.

Ms Woodruff said her legal expertise was the key to the Greater Manchester Police taking her concerns seriously when she went to them a month after her mother's death.

'Once they knew that I was a lawyer, it became much easier,' Ms Woodruff said. 'I suppose I was more likely to be objective being a solicitor. I also realised the seriousness of the case straight away.'

And serious it was. The investigation started as one into possible forgery and an attempt to obtain monies by deception. Who knew this would unearth Britain's most prolific serial killer?

When Mrs Grundy's body was exhumed, police toxicologists found a large dose of diamorphine. Shipman, who denied killing anyone, suggested Mrs Grundy could have been a secret drug addict. In his police interview regarding Mrs Grundy, Shipman stated: '…I have said that I had my suspicions that she was abusing a narcotic of some sort, or at least taking a narcotic of some sort over a period of a year or so…I am not suggesting she took drugs every day. Far from it. But the scenario was there. She did have drugs available and she may well have accidentally given herself an overdose…'

In 1970s, when he was a young doctor at a medical centre in the West Yorkshire town of Todmorden, Shipman became addicted to pethidine. A local chemist noticed Shipman signed a lot of prescriptions for the drug and made a complaint, which resulted in his colleagues forcing his resignation from the practice. Shipman admitted 75 drug offences and was fined by a magistrates' court. His colleagues arranged for him to spend time at a psychiatric hospital. In their minds, the young GP's career was over. However, Shipman returned to medical practice in 1977, where he ended up in Hyde. By now, Shipman and his wife had three children. The General Medical Council never took any disciplinary action over his criminal conviction and this left Shipman to return to medical practice with no restrictions.

Shipman was a one-man GP practice for the last six years of his medical career from 1992. He was fond of making home visits. It was a point of professional pride that he was in such demand. He had more than 3000 patients on his practice's books and a long waiting list. His wife Primrose worked as the surgery's receptionist.

With his sole practice, Shipman had even more freedom to kill. There was a pattern to his crimes – most of his victims lived alone, they were 'found' (often by Shipman) dead in their day clothes, many sitting in a favourite chair, and most died in the afternoon. Five of Shipman's known victims died in his surgery. Shipman's arrogance meant he never really expected he would be caught.

On one home visit to victim Maria West on 6 March 1995, he did not know that her friend Marion Hadfield had dropped in for a cup of tea, and was also at the house. Manners and discretion meant that Mrs Hadfield remained in the bathroom, where she had been when Shipman arrived. When she entered the living room after what seemed to be a lingering silence from Mrs West, she found Mrs West unconscious. Shipman proclaimed that 'she collapsed on me'. According to *The Shipman Inquiry*'s first report called 'Death Disguised', which detailed all the victims and the circumstances of their deaths:

> *Mrs Hadfield asked if he could do anything for her. He said it was too late; she had 'gone'. Mrs Hadfield went into the living room and found Mrs West sitting in the chair exactly where she had been before. Shipman did not attempt resuscitation. He just raised Mrs West's eyelid and said there was no sign of life...*

Shipman was devious. He falsified computer records to add symptoms for his patients that supported the cause of death he recorded. He stockpiled supplies of the drug, often on prescription under the names of dead patients. There was a pharmacy next door to his practice and he formed a close working relationship with the female pharmacist Ghislaine Brant, who never questioned his unusual and high demand for the drug.

The *Manchester Evening News* reported in October 2007 that 'on one occasion he obtained 12,000 milligrams – enough to kill 400 patients not used to diamorphine – from a single prescription for a patient who was already dead.'

Ms Brant later told an inquiry into Shipman's crimes that she never queried his prescriptions because he was a 'caring, professional GP' and she 'trusted him to use the drug appropriately'.

In the end it was greed that tripped up the arrogant doctor when he decided to forge Mrs Grundy's will. It's not clear why Shipman did this because avarice was not a pattern in his offending. It is believed he stole trinkets and jewellery from some of his victims, but financial gain was not a prime motivation for killing them. It emerged that several relatives and friends had lingering suspicions that Shipman had killed their loved ones but never reported anything because they feared they would not be believed. Who would go against the word of a respected, in many cases, much-loved and revered family doctor?

There had actually been a prior investigation into Shipman, sparked by the concerns of the GPs who were at the medical centre across the street from Shipman's practice. They were worried about the number of cremation certificates they were being asked to co-sign by Shipman (two signatures were required for these certificates). Shipman's patient death rate was also 10 times higher than theirs.

In March 1998, a secret police investigation was launched but was ultimately unsuccessful in finding any evidence that Shipman was killing his patients.

Frank Massey & Son funeral director Debbie Bambroffe was another person who had serious concerns about the number of deaths coming from Shipman's surgery.

In the Channel 5 documentary *Doctor Death*, Ms Bambroffe explained why she had been worried.

'Most of the deaths seemed to fit into a pattern. Usually ladies, almost always ladies [and] never anyone who had been ill, as in terminally ill,' Ms Bambroffe explained.

Ms Bambroffe then shared a chilling insight that, in the light of what is now known about Shipman, seems so obvious a clue that something was amiss.

'It seemed strange that nearly all the people who had died were dressed. Now if somebody's ill, they're generally usually in bed with their nightwear on. Well, that was never the case. They were always fully dressed as if they'd just come back from shopping; it was very rare that anyone actually died in bed. It was usually sat up in the chair in the living room.'

Ms Bambroffe was herself a patient of Shipman, who was so well respected and so adept at manipulation that he made Ms Bambroffe question her own professional judgment. She started to think how wrong she had been. Ms Bambroffe had also shared her concerns with her father Alan Massey. Mr Massey visited Shipman in person and was matter-of-factly assured by Shipman that he was open to anyone viewing the death certificates of his patients.

With their concerns 'eased' by Shipman, and also the people conducting the first investigation (Mr Massey and his daughter were told that Shipman had more elderly patients and it had been a bad winter), Ms Bambroffe said she put her 'ridiculous' thoughts behind her and continued to see Dr Shipman as a patient.

'The longer I sat in his room, the more ridiculous these suspicions and concerns had been. It was impossible to think that my doctor who I trusted in and confided in could be doing something so terrible,' she said.

By now, Shipman must have been aware that there were suspicions about his practices; however, he killed three more patients between March and June 1998. Some thought that Shipman's forgery of Mrs Grundy's will was a sign that he knew the spotlight was on him and that he needed money to escape and start a new life.

Shipman was arrested on 7 September 1998 for the murder of Kathleen Grundy and went on trial a year later for the killing of 15 elderly patients.

Between his arrest and trial, the police investigation into the doctor was intense. A shocking can of rancid worms had been opened up and police were determined to find the truth about this small town doctor's activities.

Exhumations played a vital role in the case. In the middle of the night over several weeks, a sensitive and unprecedented exhumation of 12 graves was conducted.

The youngest victim of the 15 deaths Shipman was charged with was that of 49-year-old Bianka Pomfret.

Ms Pomfret died on 10 December 1997. She had a long history of mental illness and depression and had been treated by Shipman for many years. On the day of her death, Shipman was due to make a house call because Ms Pomfret was 'chesty' and suffering respiratory infection symptoms. Later that day, at around 5pm, a community mental health support worker arrived for a scheduled appointment but could not rouse Ms Pomfret to the door. Peering through the window, the worker could see Ms Pomfret on the sofa. Ms Pomfret's son William was called to open the door and he found his mother dead. According to *The Shipman Inquiry*'s first report, Ms Pomfret 'was fully clothed and looked relaxed. A half-drunk cup of coffee and a burned out cigarette were on the table beside her.'

When the paramedics arrived they called Dr Shipman and he confirmed he had visited Ms Pomfret at 12.30pm and she had complained of chest pains. Shipman said he had advised his patient to make another appointment and that she had refused medication and other tests. He told the family that Ms Pomfret must have had a heart attack sometime in the afternoon. On the medical certificate Shipman stated that death was due to coronary thrombosis with heart disease as an underlying cause.

The police investigations later revealed that Shipman had two completely different accounts of his actions that day. He told Ms Pomfret's psychiatrist that he found her collapsed and attempted resuscitation and defibrillation to no avail.

Shipman had also backdated his records in the days after Ms Pomfret's death to show a history of chest pain. This was another facet of his modus operandi. He falsified medical records on his computer. However clever he purported to be though, Shipman did not really give thought to the fact that a computer hard drive would record when he made changes to the records system.

The body of Ms Pomfret was exhumed in 1998 and a post mortem found the morphine levels in her tissues must have come from a fatal dose of the drug. The coroner could not find any sign of heart disease, as Dr Shipman had documented, and also found that the morphine must have been given to her while she was alive.

On 31 January 2000 at the Preston Crown Court, Shipman was convicted of murder in the 15 cases.

As he handed down Shipman's 15 life sentences, Judge Thayne Forbes said, 'You are a wicked, wicked man. Each of your victims was your patient and you killed each and every one of your victims by a calculated and cold-blooded perversion of your medical skills.

'You were, after all, each victim's doctor. I have no doubt that each of your victims smiled and thanked you as she submitted to your deadly administrations. Yours was not a healing touch. None of them knew that it brought them death, which was disguised as the caring attention of a good doctor.'

Shipman was jailed at Wakefield Prison, in West Yorkshire. On 13 January 2004, he committed suicide by hanging himself in his cell.

Father Denis Maher had been a Catholic parish priest in Hyde since 1996 and became an unofficial spokesman for the victims' families. On the evening of Shipman's guilty verdict he spoke to Channel 4's Krishnan Guru-Murthy, who was on location in the town, about the reaction to the convictions.

'A lot of questions have to be asked about how this could have happened. How this went on for so long,' Father Maher said.

'[There's] a lot of anger. People feel very much…people in the parish and in the community feel let down by people who ought to be keeping a check. How come nobody ever seemed to have inquired why there were so many sudden deaths among Dr Shipman's patients?'

Father Maher had first met Shipman when he was called to the home of victim Winifred Mellor, who had died suddenly on 11 May 1998. Mrs Mellor's family was distraught and wanted the support of the parish priest.

Father Maher said he was shocked by Shipman's unfeeling, almost callous attitude to Mrs Mellor's death. Something wasn't right. Months later, Father Maher would attend the exhumation of Mrs Mellor's body, and the several others that occurred as part of the investigation. Exhumations are not a common occurrence with around four conducted each year in the United Kingdom. This figure tripled during the investigation into Shipman.

Later, after Shipman's suicide, Father Maher told the *Catholic Herald* that the townsfolk had hoped their once trusted family doctor would have a change of heart and tell them why he killed so many people.

'He had a manner which earned him a reputation as a good family doctor. He became a friend to many families, and he would call round to their houses to see how they were. Looking back, this was his stock in trade. Because of that, he was able to get away with it for so long. He was very nice to people as long as they went along with what he said,' Father Maher told the *Catholic Herald* for the January 23, 2004 article.

Detective Superintendent Bernard Postles, who led the police investigation into Shipman, told BBC crime correspondent Stephen Cape on the day of the evil doctor's conviction that he was surprised Shipman was not caught earlier.

'I am surprised that people were unable to, shall we say, put two and two together,' Postles said, 'because it became apparent at a later stage when people began to ring in, that as they started to hear parts of the story that they realised that some of the concerns that they had had a year or two before in some cases, were very, very similar.'

Postles said that when the initial story about Kathleen Grundy's death was publicised, the police started to get calls from the public.

'Some of these people had harboured concerns about the death of their relative for quite some time, in some cases years,' he recalled for the program *Police Story: Investigating Shipman*.

The British Government swiftly established *The Shipman Inquiry* in 2001 following the doctor's conviction. To date, it is one of the most significant inquiries in British history.

The inquiry, headed by Dame Janet Smith, then a high court judge, found that Shipman murdered 218 of his patients and that there was a 'real suspicion' that he had killed up to 250 and had started the murders when he was just 25 and fresh out of medical school.

The Shipman Inquiry was divided into two parts, which examined the victims of Shipman and the manner of their deaths, then the failings of the various systems that should have identified his crimes. The inquiry released six reports over the almost four years of the investigations with the last one released in January 2005.

The inquiry into Shipman after his conviction found that 'two detectives from Greater Manchester police, who carried out an initial, failed investigation into Harold Shipman in March 1998, were inexperienced and unfit for the case'. The detective inspector of the first inquiry also came in for criticism as it was found that, among other failings, he never checked if Shipman had any prior convictions.

Most of Shipman's victims were women. However, despite a perception that Shipman only targeted lone women, there were at least 44 men that the inquiry identified were unlawfully killed by Shipman.

The inquiry decided to place an advertisement in newspapers around the country, including the *Manchester Evening News* and *The Sun*. It was quite a bold decision but one that was invaluable to the inquiry's efforts to find the truth about Shipman and, in particular, 82 people whose death certificates had been signed by the doctor. Included in the list of 82 possible victims were 19 people from one nursing home.

Shipman's victims were mostly elderly – the oldest was 93-year-old Ann Cooper – but it is believed his youngest was 42-year-old Peter Lewis. Mr Lewis died in January 1985. He had stomach cancer that Shipman did not diagnose for six months after he began to show symptoms. In her statement to *The Shipman Inquiry*, Mr Lewis's widow Muriel Hamilton said Shipman had insisted an ulcer caused her husband's condition. Mrs Hamilton (who remarried in the years after her husband's death) said she had called Shipman for a home visit because Peter was so ill. His mother was also there and the pair saw Shipman give him a needle.

Distraught, Mrs Hamilton left the room but her mother-in-law, Elsie Gee saw Shipman attempting to smother Peter with a pillow.

'Dr Shipman was standing by the bed in front of Peter holding a pillow in both hands. He was putting the pillow over Peter's face,' Mrs Gee told the inquiry in 2002, as reported in the *Manchester Evening News*.

'I shrieked, "What are you doing, man?" and he put the pillow at the back of Peter's neck,' Mrs Gee said.

Mrs Hamilton said she wasn't in the room when Peter died but the *Manchester Evening News* reported that she wrote in her inquiry statement that she overheard Shipman say, 'Come on lad, give up. We've all had enough.'

'I gained the impression he was willing him to die,' Mrs Hamilton wrote.

Another victim, Bertha Moss, 68, died in Shipman's surgery when she went for a regular diabetes check on 13 June 1995. *The Shipman Inquiry* notified her children in 2002 that their mother had been unlawfully killed by the GP she had trusted for over 20 years.

Bertha Moss's family also received a separate letter concerning the death of their father, Mrs Moss's first husband, Sydney Walton, 52, who died at home after a visit from Shipman in 1979. The inquiry had decided it was inconclusive whether Shipman had killed their father.

One daughter, Joan Clayton, who had moved to Brisbane, Australia, said, 'It's pretty awful to think somebody could have cold-bloodedly killed both your parents. It's horrific.'

In an interview with Queensland newspaper the *Sunday Mail* in 2002, Mrs Clayton said her mother's untimely death was a dreadful shock.

'She hadn't been ill – I'd been talking to her a couple of days before she died,' Mrs Clayton told journalist Kay Dibben.

After her mother's death, Mrs Clayton made a swift dash to England to grieve with her siblings. She said she even went to Dr Shipman's surgery for an explanation of what had happened.

'He convinced me that she had a massive heart attack and he had tried to revive her,' Mrs Clayton said. 'It never entered my head that he could have done that.'

The inquiry also revealed that Shipman killed two women within four hours of each other. On 24 February 1993, Shipman made home visits to Olive Heginbotham, 86, and Hilda Couzens, 92. Both women were later found dead at their homes.

There is just one known survivor of Shipman who, when publicity of the case emerged, realised she came perilously close to being murdered by the then-young doctor. University professor Elaine Oswald read about Shipman's crimes from her home in America and her blood ran cold remembering the time, when she was just 25, that she had almost died.

Ms Oswald lived in Todmorden and went to see Shipman with symptoms of stomach pain in August 1974. Shipman said he would visit her home to take blood samples and asked her to leave the door unlocked.

A June 2001 article in *The Telegraph* titled 'The Killing Fields of Harold Shipman' recounted Elaine Oswald's near-death experience as she told it to *The Shipman Inquiry*. Ms Oswald said the last memory she had was of Shipman coming near her with a needle in his hand.

'The next thing I know, I'm lying on the floor. There are a lot of people in my bedroom. My mouth's bleeding, there's blood trickling down my mouth. I can't breathe; my ribs are hurting every time I breathe. The people in the room are shaking me, slapping my face. All I wanted to do was sleep, just sleep for ever.'

The people in the room were paramedics and Shipman's wife and their young son. Shipman told Ms Oswald she must have suffered an allergic reaction to the shot and he saved her life. How Primrose Shipman came to be at the house was unclear but Shipman told her to call an ambulance. Shipman even visited Ms Oswald in hospital and she thought of him as her lifesaver.

After speaking at the inquiry, Mrs Oswald said, 'I firmly believe Shipman tried to kill me. He's evil. I'm the only one who can speak for all the dead women.'

The first report of *The Shipman Inquiry*, 'Death Disguised', was released on 19 July 2002. A church bell in Hyde tolled 215 times, once for each of the identified victims of Shipman.

At the time *The Shipman Inquiry* began, Elaine Oswald was thought to be Shipman's first intended victim. However, the inquiry investigated Shipman's activities at West Yorkshire's Pontefract General Infirmary (PGI), where he went for a compulsory period of employment as a house officer from August 1970 to July 1971, after he graduated from the University of Leeds' School of Medicine. After the requisite year as a house officer, junior doctors obtain full registration. Shipman stayed on at the hospital until early 1974.

According to *The Shipman Inquiry*'s sixth report, 'Shipman: The Final Report', Mrs Sandra Whitehead (formerly Goddard) contacted the police a few days after Shipman had been found dead in his prison cell in January 2004. Mrs Whitehead was a student nurse at the PGI between 1971 and 1974 and when she had read of Shipman's death, she remembered that the pair had worked together briefly. She expressed concern to the inquiry office that Shipman may have been killing patients during that time. The terms of reference of the inquiry meant that Mrs

Whitehead's concerns had to be followed up and the inquiry team interviewed her.

Though it was a long time ago, Mrs Whitehead recalled she did not enjoy her time on Ward 1 at the hospital, where she and Shipman both worked for a time. As a young nurse, death on the ward makes an impression and Mrs Whitehead recalled there were a lot of deaths on the ward.

'She remembered that, on many occasions when a patient had died, there would be an empty injection pack by the bed, indicating that an injection had been administered shortly before death...' the report stated.

Mrs Whitehead told investigators that once she made the connection that Shipman worked at the hospital she instinctively knew he had been killing patients.

'I felt I just knew he had been killing patients on that ward and it explained for me why there had been such a high death rate,' Mrs Whitehead said.

Her suspicions were confirmed in that the death rate on that particular ward was high at the time, and a review of patient records was undertaken. The inquiry decided not to inform families of the deceased whose records were being looked at until it was established that there was cause for concern. On the preliminary advice of University of Leicester's Professor Richard Baker who examined the records, there *was* cause for concern and further investigation. Not only had Shipman worked on Ward 1, but he had also worked in the paediatric wing, the obstetrics and gynaecology department and several other wards of the hospital.

With the help of the local press and investigators, the inquiry managed to find 'at least one member of the family (or a friend) of 117 of the 137 deceased patients' and 162 witness statements were made.

The statements of medical staff – doctors and nurses – who worked with Shipman during those years at the PGI vacillated between reports of him being 'keen and energetic', 'a nice, caring young man', 'confident and conscientious', 'a loner personality', 'felt he knew better than anybody else' and 'arrogant'.

In her report, Dame Janet Smith said the impressions of Shipman garnered from the witness statements of former colleagues 'are of real interest and value in building up an overall portrait of him as a young man'.

'Some of the characteristics described during this early period were also to be found in the mature man and were essential features underlying his criminality...'

A characteristic mentioned was Shipman's habit of ingratiating himself with senior staff, especially nurses:

> *Some regarded him as strange, sinister and odd. These people were in the minority; the majority admired him. A very similar pattern was to be found later. Most people admired and respected him; some colleagues found him difficult, arrogant and 'prickly'. In short, the evidence about Shipman as a young professional in Pontefract is entirely consistent with the picture of the mature GP in Hyde.*

Dr Baker found that there were three patients who were unlawfully killed by Shipman in April and May 1972. Based on Dr Baker's work, Dame Smith found there were three other deaths that gave rise to serious suspicion and 13 others caused some suspicion for him.

One of the deaths that Dr Baker found suspicious was that of four-year-old Susie Garfitt. Susie had cerebral palsy and severe epilepsy and was admitted to hospital with a serious chest infection. There were no medical records or cremation certificates for Susie, who died in 1973. Dr Baker's findings were based on his interviews with Susie's mother, Ann, about what happened on her little girl's last admission to hospital.

Mrs Garfitt said a nice doctor (who was most likely Shipman) explained that Susie was very unwell and, while they could treat her with strong doses of medication, the girl's prognosis was poor. Mrs Garfitt said she told the doctor to 'be kind' to Susie. She recalled she went away for 10 minutes for a cup of tea and when she returned Susie was dead.

She explained to Dr Baker that she never gave permission for the doctor to do anything to speed up her daughter's death and had not expected Susie to die so soon.

'I was shocked Susie died so quickly. Although I knew that she was dying I did not think her death was imminent,' Mrs Garfitt said.

Dame Smith felt it entirely likely that Shipman was the doctor who treated Susie and that he may have administered a fatal injection to the little girl to hasten her death.

'Shipman seemed to think that he knew when the right time had come for some patients to die. It is entirely possible that he had taken that view with Susie Garfitt,' Dame Smith said in the report.

In the final Shipman inquiry report, Dame Smith said, 'My overall conclusion is that Shipman killed about 250 patients between 1971 and 1998, of whom I have been able positively to identify 218.'

It was the contact by Mrs Whitehead that led to a far clearer picture of Shipman's offences. Often more is revealed when just one person makes the bold step to speak up, even if they fear they will be dismissed. Dame Smith made special thanks to her for her actions:

> *I would like to express my thanks to Mrs Whitehead for drawing her concerns to the attention of the police and for assisting the Inquiry. As will later appear, her concerns were not without foundation and, if it were not for her action in coming forward, the Inquiry's investigations would have been incomplete.*

There is informed speculation about what motivated Shipman to kill. When he was a teenager, his beloved mother Vera had cancer and died at age 43. Shipman witnessed the slow and very painful death his mother endured – and the frequent injections of diamorphine that she was given by her doctor to ease the pain. Then there was the fact that he was a drug addict early on in his career. Could that have been the reason?

Certainly the evidence from people who knew Shipman and worked with him give a picture of a manipulative personality who could be charming and nice but then egotistical and raging with fury. An unpredictable yet functioning addict?

Shipman likely enjoyed the power he had over his patients. Dr Ian Napier, who worked with Shipman at a practice during the 1980s, recalled that Shipman had two sides – charming and pleasant but also rude, arrogant and with a volatile temper that would explode every few months.

Dr Napier told *The Guardian* for a February 2000 feature 'The Doctor

Jekyll of Hyde' that 'if crossed, he was capable of making people's lives a misery'.

'Although he was an excellent clinician, he could be volatile and bombastic; but when he was nice, he was very nice…I remember on one occasion he reduced a drug company representative, who had only been in the job for two weeks, to tears. He was a funny sort of devil.'

The forensic psychiatrist who examined Shipman, Dr Richard Badcock, thought Shipman could have enjoyed some sort of sexual gratification from causing death. Dr Badcock believed Shipman showed symptoms of a 'classic necrophiliac'. He said the sexual gratification came not from having sex with a dead body (as most people would believe necrophilia entails) but from controlling and watching the moment when life leaves the body.

It has also been suggested that the way Shipman murdered his victims – often while they were sitting in an armchair – was a replication over and over again of the lasting image of his seriously ill and dying mother with whom he had a very close relationship.

Taking part in the documentary *Doctor Death*, world-renowned professor of forensic toxicology Robert Forrest gave his take on why he thought Shipman killed. Professor Forrest gave evidence at Shipman's trial and has been an expert in several other high-profile cases including the 2008 inquest into the death of Princess Diana. (He said on 22 January 2008 that problems with the blood samples from the body of Princess Diana's driver Henri Paul suggested a 'conspiracy or a cock-up'.)

'Why he [Shipman] did it is simply a matter of convenience. It was more convenient, perhaps, to get rid of a patient, who was an awkward patient, by killing her than by trying to persuade the family practitioner committee to transfer her to another general practitioner. It's horrendous, isn't it, to think that that could happen but it clearly did. I think that a significant number of the people that Dr Shipman killed he may have killed quite simply because he did not wish to continue caring for them for whatever reason.'

Another baffling aspect of Shipman's crimes is whether his widow Primrose knew more than she claimed. When police questioned her during the investigation, Mrs Shipman simply said she wasn't sure what went on (this response was strange since she was receptionist at the practice).

In a 14 January 2004 *Daily Mail* article, journalist and author Geoffrey Wansell wrote about Primrose Shipman's complete denial about her husband's evil deeds. (Wansell is well-versed in examining crimes and criminals and wrote the best-selling biography on the depraved killer Fred West called *An Evil Love*.)

Wansell proposed that Mrs Shipman suffered from a rare psychological condition known as folie à deux. The condition is defined by the *Diagnostic and Statistical Manual of Mental Disorders* as a rare delusional disorder shared by two people with close emotional ties.

Mrs Shipman was a dowdy, grossly overweight woman and never spoke to the media. She was reported to be a virtual prisoner in the cottage she lived in, which was an hour's drive from her husband's Wakefield Prison home.

Having married Shipman when she was just 17 (and pregnant with their first child), Primrose Shipman was a somewhat sheltered woman, totally devoted to her marriage and children. In fact, her shotgun wedding upset her strict Methodist parents and their relationship became strained. She had to believe that her marriage was worth the sacrifice she had made as a young girl and she became an extremely dutiful wife. The shame of Shipman's drug addiction and court fines was the breaking point for her tenuous relationship with her parents. Primrose was devoted to 'Fred' (the name she called her husband) and cared for the children while he studied, worked and spent his free time as a member of a local canal restoration society and a volunteer for St John Ambulance.

British Relationship psychologist Corinne Sweet wrote a comment piece in *The Guardian* on 16 January 2004 titled 'He could do no wrong': 'Friends say that Shipman was everything to his wife and that she was devoted and submissive to a man commonly remembered as moody and domineering. He has been described by many as forceful, clever, enigmatic; she was barely literate and highly impressionable…'

In another article in *The Telegraph* on 18 January 2004, Dr Sweet was quoted speaking about the life of Mrs Shipman in the wake of her husband's suicide.

'We will now displace on to her our hatred for Shipman, and we hate women a lot more than we hate men,' Dr Sweet said. 'We find it very difficult to stomach when a woman, a mother, supports a murderer.'

'Denial is a self-defence mechanism. If Primrose really acknowledged to herself what had happened, it would destroy her...'

Any hope for a confession or an explanation for the hundreds of people he killed died in a prison cell with Shipman on 13 January 2004. The serial killer committed suicide by hanging in his cell at Wakefield Prison. He was 57. The next day was his birthday.

Head of the police inquiry into Shipman, Bernard Postles, who by now had retired from the Greater Manchester Police, said the doctor's death was deeply frustrating for families and friends of the victims.

'For the last four years they have held out some hope he would tell them the reasoning behind these offences,' Postles said.

The Sun newspaper, famous for its controversial front pages, produced the headline 'SHIP SHIP HOORAY' to announce the doctor's death. The newspaper was criticised by some pundits and politicians for its gleefulness at Shipman's death but many thought it was entirely appropriate. The then home secretary David Blunkett controversially admitted that he felt like celebrating when he got the call that Shipman had killed himself.

'You wake up and you receive a phone call – Shipman's topped himself. You have just got to think for a minute: is it too early to open a bottle? And then you discover that everybody's very upset that he's done it,' Mr Blunkett said, realising the families of the victims were cheated out of an explanation for their loved ones' deaths.

Mr Blunkett made the frank comments at a Westminster lunch for London-based regional journalists just a few days after Shipman's death.

Shipman was reportedly cremated in a private ceremony.

The Sun reported that Mrs Shipman had wanted a burial for her husband and that at least one undertaker had refused to be involved in the disposal of his body. The newspaper also quoted an unnamed source from Wakefield Prison who said Mrs Shipman was strongly advised that a gravesite could be a target for vandals or for desecration.

There were some revelations after Shipman's death from people who claimed he had confided in them.

The Sun bagged an exclusive two days after Shipman's death when a fellow inmate, whom the deadly doctor had confided in, revealed some of his secrets.

Andrew McEwan, who spent some time with Shipman in Manchester Prison in 2000, was trained by the charitable organisation The Samaritans to be a 'listener' for fellow prisoners.

McEwan, who had served two years for assault, told the newspaper that Shipman quietly told him that he had lost count how many people he had killed.

'He always had an air of arrogance,' McEwan told *The Sun*.

'He kept talking about the power he had. He said he had the ability to take a life whenever he fancied – the power of life and death made him do it.'

McEwan also said that Shipman revealed he would eventually kill himself.

'In one session he said, "I'm going to top myself – there's no way I'm spending my life in prison. All this is going to the grave with me,"' McEwan said.

An 18 January 2004 exclusive by the *Sunday Times*, which obtained 14 letters that Shipman had written to a former neighbour and family friend Shirley Horsfall while in jail, suggested that it was feelings of 'inadequacy, anger and wounded pride' that prompted the suicide. The letters revealed Shipman's arrogance and inability to feel any guilt over his crimes.

Ms Horsfall lived next door to Shipman in Todmorden and her late father, Ben, even acted as a character witness for the young doctor when he was under threat of being struck off the professional register after his addiction to pethidine was revealed in 1975.

In one letter to Ms Horsfall, Shipman described prison life: 'The place is full of thieves, I get all the nutters asking me how I did it, how much money did I get and so on...'

In another, Shipman uncharacteristically revealed a vulnerable side: 'The problem is for 30 years plus I've had the professional mask of a doctor. Now I'm me. Who am I? No ideas yet. I find it emotionally very odd...'

Shipman was also scathing of the police and blamed them for his predicament. 'All those [witnesses] so carefully rehearsed by the police. Why they just didn't have a recording to play each time and just change the name?'

In 2005, an inquiry into his death found the serial killer's suicide could not have been predicted or prevented by prison officers. The prison's ombudsman, Stephen Shaw, said even though Shipman had some of his jailhouse privileges revoked in late 2003 (because Shipman had refused to take part in some offender rehabilitation courses), these had been reinstated in the days before his death.

The inquest also heard that another likely motivation for taking his own life was that Primrose Shipman would be entitled to a widow's pension if he died before 60. The government had stopped his GP's pension, but the widow's component of this was not affected.

Over the course of the few years he had been in prison, Shipman had made some mentions of taking his own life, and had been placed on suicide watch but had not spoken of it since being moved to Wakefield Prison in mid-2003. A criticism during the inquiry was of the way information on suicide risks was passed from prison to prison. Basically, Wakefield Prison had not been told that their infamous prisoner had made previous suicide threats.

There were sweeping recommendations for the healthcare profession that arose from *The Shipman Inquiry*, which cost £20 million of taxpayers' money.

Some key findings were that disciplinary and criminal records of doctors should be held centrally and shared with healthcare organisations, checks for abnormally high death rates at GP practices needed to be undertaken, and dedicated advice and support networks should be set up for National Health Service (NHS) staff and the public to make complaints.

A major change that occurred after the Shipman case was new regulations for cremation. The Cremation (England and Wales)

Regulations were introduced on 1 January 2009. Before these new regulations, if a relative applied for cremation of their loved one, a second doctor was required to fill out a new certificate to confirm the cause of death. The new system gave families the right to look at the medical forms of a deceased relative before a cremation could take place.

Shipman's evil deeds also exposed weaknesses in death certification. Time and time again it was found that there was a conflict of evidence where Shipman claimed he offered the families a post mortem for their loved ones, but they refused. Many of the families said this was not the case. Also as a doctor, he should have declined to sign the death certificate if he was not confident of the actual cause of death. It was not his place to offer a post-mortem examination.

Could this happen again? Could there be another Harold Shipman?

People involved in the case say, regrettably, yes.

Some believe the Shipman case should be compulsorily taught in medical schools across Britain.

One professor Aneez Esmail told the BBC in 2009 that medical students must understand what happened and the subsequent implications for the profession.

'What really worried me was firstly how little people knew about him, and I find this incredible. Here is a doctor that should stand out as something we all have to know about...because this is what happened on our watch, our profession,' Professor Esmail said.

Perhaps the difficulty in identifying healthcare serial killers is best summed up by another Hyde GP Raj Patel, who, as a young locum, worked for Shipman. Patel was one of five GPs at the Brooke Surgery across the street from Shipman's practice.

Dr Patel said, 'You can legislate against a poor doctor but you can't legislate against evil.'

www.ingramcontent.com/pod-product-compliance
Lightning Source LLC
Chambersburg PA
CBHW030925090426
42737CB00007B/325